WHAT SEX IS DEATH?

Dario Bellezza, 1982, Siracusa (used with permission of the Archivio Centrale dello Stato, Archivio Massimo Consoli)

WHAT SEX IS DEATH?

Dario Bellezza

Selected and translated by Peter Covino

THE UNIVERSITY OF WISCONSIN PRESS

Publication of this book has been made possible, in part,
through support from the Brittingham Trust.

The University of Wisconsin Press
728 State Street, Suite 443
Madison, Wisconsin 53706
uwpress.wisc.edu

Printed in the United States of America

Library of Congress Cataloging-in-Publication Data

Names: Bellezza, Dario, author. | Covino, Peter, translator. | Bellezza, Dario.
What sex is death? | Bellezza, Dario. What sex is death? English
Title: What sex is death? / Dario Bellezza ; selected and translated by Peter Covino.
Other titles: What sex is death? (Compilation)
Description: Madison, Wisconsin : The University of Wisconsin Press, 2025. |
Series: Wisconsin poetry series | Selections from Invettive e licenze (1971),
Morte segreta (1976), Libro d'amore (1982), io (1983), Serpenta (1987),
Libro di poesia (1990), L'avversario (1994), and Proclama sul fascino (1996). |
Includes bibliographical references.
Identifiers: LCCN 2024039060 | ISBN 9780299350345 (paperback)
Subjects: LCSH: Bellezza, Dario—Translations into English. | LCGFT: Poetry.
Classification: LCC PQ4862.E38 W4713 2025 | DDC 851/.914—dc23/eng/20240911
LC record available at https://lccn.loc.gov/2024039060

Contents

Introduction

Oltraggio e scandalo—(Out)rage and Scandal

At the precocious age of twenty-six, poet, novelist, and playwright Dario Bellezza (1944–96) published his daring, debut poetry collection, *Invettive e licenze* (*Invective and License*, 1971), which was hailed for its ability to "dig deeper within the Piranesian ruins to the vital zones of inertia where morality begins to stammer out its credo."[1] Twentieth-century Italian literary luminaries Pier Paolo Pasolini, Alberto Moravia, and Elsa Morante, among others, further championed Bellezza's work. Over the course of a twenty-five-year publishing career, Bellezza published more than twenty books, including eight full-length poetry collections, eight novels, two plays, translations from the French, and two exposés about Pasolini's gruesome murder.[2] In addition to *Invettive e licenze* (1971, reprinted 1992), which won the Gatti Prize, other notable works include *Morte segreta* (*Secret Death*, 1976) winner of the Viareggio Prize, Italy's most prestigious poetry recognition; and *L'avversario* (*The Adversary*, 1994), which won the Montale Prize for lifetime poetic achievement.

Despite early and consistent accolades, as the work of an openly gay writer who died a premature death of AIDS-related illness, Bellezza's poetry remained marginalized for years, even as reader interest endured. A documentary film, *Bellezza addio* (2023), about his life recently premiered to stellar reviews and a first commercial biography is imminent.[3] Yet, until Mondadori's *Dario Bellezza, Tutte le poesie* (*Collected Poems*, 2015) edited by Roberto Deidier, all of Bellezza's poetry books were out of print and painstaking to track down, though widely coveted, especially by poetry aficionados and members of the international LGBTQ+

community. In a late interview, Bellezza tells a close friend who helped care for him at the end of his long illness that "he regretted not cultivating enough contacts to ensure his poetry was even better known abroad."[4] *What Sex Is Death?* attempts to fulfill Bellezza's desire for a wider audience by contextualizing and providing English translations of some seventy of the most representative poems of this brave queer work, collected in one volume for the first time.

When I first encountered Bellezza's poetry, I was one of those identity-questing, overprivileged study-abroad students that Bellezza frequently rails against in his writing. Urbane post-boom Rome of the 1980s was a far cry from the isolated southern Italian mountain village in the province of Avellino my parents had fled a decade or so earlier. Prosperity had still to reach many poor and working-class Italian families. The mid-1970s marked the end of an arduous period of unprecedented migration that witnessed more than twenty-eight million mostly southern Italians leave Italy, nearly half the country's population, in a one-hundred-year period.[5] As an Italian American for the first time in Italy without family members, I experienced everything as chic and adventurous—an updated version of Pasolini's homoerotic Neorealism immortalized in his novel *Ragazzi di vita* (1955) and in his film *Accattone* (1961). This was at the height of Eurail travel, and I was determined to soak up as much European experience as possible between frequent missions to enjoy 900-lira (50¢) Peroni at a favorite bar sandwiched between Campo dei Fiori and Piazza Farnese in Rome's historic center, not far from Via dei Pettinari 75, where Bellezza lived most of his adult life.

Rome felt uncharted and indecipherable. Plenty of youth from the quickly industrializing Roman suburbs roughhoused and, alternately, pestered or fell in love with the growing throngs of international students and tourists. The sociocultural divide seemed lessened and, as is compellingly explored in Bellezza's work, an emerging queer sensibility and fleeting intimacy promised to be a great equalizer. Like many college students, I was in the thrall of Michel Foucault's canonical *The History of Sexuality* (1978), which was accompanied by a wide diffusion of emergent ideas of queer kinship. Bellezza grew up in a working-class section of Monteverde in Rome, and his mother was an emigrant from Taranto,

Puglia. In effect, his work participates in what has continued to emerge as a "postcolonial consciousness" in Italy that critics argue defines the "The North/South duality so central to Italy's self-identity"; that is, northern Italy's long-standing exploitation of the southern part of the country, still hindered today by its feudal economic history and pervasive corruption.[6] As a student of the *liceo classico*, high school based on classical learning models, Bellezza was knowledgeable of Greek and especially Latin literature. He never completed his university studies, however, or defended his thesis. Instead, he became a self-taught, anti-establishment iconoclast in the spirit of the celebrated French symbolist poet Arthur Rimbaud. Bellezza would go on to translate all of Rimbaud's poetry, and he considered the great precursor of modernist experimentation a major, liberating aesthetic influence. During my year abroad, I was fortunate to study Bellezza's work with the great Italian poet and novelist Giorgio Bassani, author of the gay-themed *Gli occhiali d'oro* (*The Gold-Rimmed Spectacles*, 1958); and *The Garden of the Finzi-Contini* (1965), among others, then at the height of his fame. Bassani would go on to be part of the jury that awarded Bellezza the prestigious Montale Prize.[7]

Bellezza's writing was a startling initiation; it offered queer jargon and transgressive language in my mother tongue that resonated in ways most of my Catholic family could never understand or appreciate. As Pasolini's one-time secretary, Bellezza also embodied many of his great mentor's aesthetic influences. He describes his assistantship with Pasolini as "an accelerated workout in the gymnasium of poetry."[8] Unlike Pasolini, though, Bellezza embraced his identity as an out gay man, and he was consistently supportive of gay rights causes. Significantly, Bellezza's literary career extends two decades beyond Pasolini's death, during a period of increasing visibility and polemicizing of the gay community, accompanied by a rise in socioeconomic opportunity as well as media exposure for the middle and lower classes.

Bellezza's work exhibits a keen interest in the vicissitudes and triumphs of European and international gay and queer culture writ large. In addition to his first two prizewinning poetry collections, Bellezza's provocative novels of the 1970s helped catapult his fame, but they may have also been responsible for the backlash against his work, especially the epistolary novel *Lettere da Sodoma* (*Letters from Sodom*, 1972), which portrays a relationship between a desperate older man and a teenage, drug-addicted male prostitute.[9]

Bellezza's work was indelibly influenced by poets Sandro Penna and Amelia Rosselli. Penna's sustained friendship and openly gay dalliances, in a time when this was uncommon, impact Bellezza more than Penna's delightful but, in contrast, more lyrically unified, epigrammatic poems. Bellezza and Amelia Rosselli remained friends and lived blocks from each other for their whole lives.[10] The challenges Bellezza and Rosselli faced are distressingly parallel. Just weeks before Bellezza succumbed to opportunistic infections caused by AIDS–related complications on March 31, 1996, Rosselli had committed suicide by jumping from her fifth-floor apartment on February 11, 1996, after battling serious mental illness for much of her adult life and living in great financial hardship. The two poets are buried within yards of each other in the much-visited non-Catholic cemetery in Rome. Their work represents a transnational poetics mutually influenced by the French avant-garde and mid-century experimental American poetry that is only recently beginning to be appreciated. Critics remark on the relationship between Rosselli's and Bellezza's work by noting the similarities in their "use of puns, lapses, [and innuendo] and in their lexical deconstructions and phonetic permutations."[11]

Allen Ginsberg also valued Bellezza's work, and vice versa. In 1996, when Ginsberg learned of Bellezza's worsening health and imminent death, he faxed a letter of appeal to the Italian government to help pass the Legge Bacchelli, a law offering minimal financial assistance to important cultural figures in dire need.[12] The International Gay and Lesbian Human Rights Commission, whose board members at the time included Judith Butler, among other high-profile figures, also provided a letter on Bellezza's behalf during this agonizing time of his life. Unfortunately, the law was not promulgated in time for Bellezza to benefit from it.

A Postmodern Orpheus: Early Poems and Queer Activism

The wide-ranging literary and sociocultural dimensions of Bellezza's work cannot be overestimated. I characterize his poetry as intimate Dada-surrealist–inspired lyric that integrates the most daring, urgent, and time-tested lessons of Catullus, Rimbaud, André Gide, and Allen

Ginsberg all at once, as his poem "What Sex Is Death?," which inspires this book's title, among others, attests.[13] From the onset of his career, Bellezza's proclivity for bold pronouncements and his acerbic wit link his work not only to the pithy revelations of classical writers and the brash indictments of Nietzsche but also to the quick-paced, sound-driven poetry of the Italian futurists and related avant-gardists. In Bellezza's radical, post-1968 and post-Stonewall contemporary idiom, classical themes, such as Orpheus and Eurydice's mythical search for union and rebirth, are juxtaposed against transitory and often disquieting sexual encounters and mundane cruising among proverbial "thickets." "What Sex Is Death?," written more than fifty years ago, is one of two poems included in the first section of his first published collection, *Invective and License*. The poem functions as a prologue and exhortation by announcing Bellezza's earliest challenges to bourgeois culture, gender, and sexual identity in a fearless, ironic, and impetuous style. I read this invective as an overcompensated send-up or an aggressive trope of camp performativity that conveys Bellezza's own fears and frustrations about his evolving sexuality and society's threatening lack of acceptance. At a deeper intertextual level, Bellezza's allusions suggest a powerful familiarity with the elegiac tale of Orpheus's failure to rescue Eurydice, including Orpheus's tragic death at the hands of the Ciconian women after he spurned their romantic interest.[14]

The words critics and literary friends have frequently used to describe Dario Bellezza's multifaceted work include polemical, rebellious, and simultaneously self-deprecating and theatrical.[15] The writing, "rich with raging tension," also reveals the mind of an uncompromising provocateur, one whose intent is often to incite, protest, and offend while challenging the stultifying stereotypes of a strongly politicized, emerging homosexual culture gripped by the powers of the Vatican and a deeply conservative Catholic ethos.[16] Despite the hostility and miscomprehension he faced, Bellezza would nevertheless become a major figure in Rome's organized political action on behalf of homosexual rights throughout the 1970s and until the time of his death. In addition to his political advocacy, Bellezza's scathing editorial reportages on behalf of leftist causes are further documented through his friendship with Massimo Consoli, his closest writer friend and noted gay rights activist and archivist. Consoli devotes about half of his memoir *Affetti speciali* (*Special Affects*, 1999) to his friendship with Bellezza and their "homophile revolutionary" activities, which earlier in the decade caused Consoli to flee to Amsterdam for fear of political reprisals by the right-wing government at the time. For Consoli's 1971 *Manifesto for Homosexual Rights*, Bellezza contributed a powerful essay that extols individual liberties and the psychic force of the pleasure principle.[17] Consoli and Bellezza were also early members of the Roman chapter of the Fronte Unitario Omosessuale Rivoluzionario Italiano, FUORI! (United Italian Revolutionary Homosexual Front), whose acronym means OUT!, and they figured prominently in its first congress in Rome in 1972. Consoli's efforts would essentially lead to the establishment of a gay activist social club, dubbed the "Gay House," modeled after Dada and Beat cultural happenings, located in the run-down working-class area of Testaccio in spaces that were formerly horse stables—the very working-class neighborhood Pasolini immortalized in his work. The association's short-lived modest headquarters, located next to two gay nightclubs, hosted political-action meetings, theater performances, and poetry events where Bellezza habitually read, often culminating in well-reported altercations with other performers and audience members.[18] Common themes frequently explored at these events included the Vietnam War, the women's rights movement—in Italy divorce became legal in 1970 and abortion in 1978—as well as the struggle for gay liberation. This embattled decade in Italy during the *Anni di piombo* (the Years of Lead), roughly from 1969 to the early 1980s, was also a time when protests flourished in response to right-wing extremism, including the neo-fascist bombings at the Banca Nazionale dell'Agricoltura in Piazza Fontana, Milan (December 12, 1969) and elsewhere.[19] Throughout the decade, this violence was also met with a terrifying string of kidnappings, robberies, and assassinations by the left-wing Red Brigades.

Bellezza's work shares a distinctive social consciousness with Beat-era poets who enjoyed enormous popularity in Italy. At the raucous Woodstock-inspired literary festival of Castelporziano in 1979, Bellezza was invited to read on the same program along with other Italian and internationally renowned poets such as Allen Ginsberg, Yevgeny Yevtushenko, Dacia Maraini, William Burroughs, Gregory Corso, Diane DiPrima, Anne Waldman, and LeRoi Jones (Amiri Baraka), among many others.[20] His friend Gregory Corso had also, by then, been living in Italy intermittently. The Beat influences are notable in the headlong rhythms and bold subject matter in many of Bellezza's poems, even though he remained skeptical about how some ideas that inspired the Beats and related Italian pop artists of the time would translate into Italian poetry, given its weighted lyric and epic traditions.[21] Nonetheless, the sexual directness and the farsighted sense of the risks gay people faced, and the improvisational, rhythmic insistence of many of the early poems, seem indebted to Ginsberg in particular, who was quickly identified as a key figure in the gay rights movements in Europe. Bellezza also believed some of Corso's "best poetry would outlive his vagabond era," and he respected Corso's "modern ability to speak to new generations" [of readers] within an emerging creative culture.[22]

Bellezza's earlier poetry directly responds to the circumscribed and homophobic Roman culture of the day, where homosexual sex was, at considerable personal risk, often constrained to the cruisy, darkened banks of the Tiber, or among "ill-illumined" public monuments and leafy shrubbery in city parks. "Colosseo" ("Coliseum") and "All'Ambra Jovinelli" ("At the Amber Palace)" are two longer tour de forces that illustrate Bellezza's discourse on an emerging gay identity in an amplified and sustained way. The Coliseum during this period was an un-gated, popular nighttime cruising area, while the Ambra Jovinelli regularly screened porn that attracted a gay clientele. Cruisy movie theaters in his day, such as the Ambra Jovinelli, would also become the setting for extended scenes in Bellezza's later, gay-themed novels.

Both "At the Amber Palace" and "Coliseum" are uncannily filmic. The minotaur as a figure of labyrinthine, Dantesque judgment and menacing condemnation in the former recalls Pasolini's satyr in his film *Medea* (1969), whereas "Coliseum," in its sweeping, nonredemptive sexualized vision, is much like the work of another famous twenty-something of the era, director Bernardo Bertolucci. Bertolucci was a friend and collaborator on Pasolini's films and the son of the well-known poet Attilio Bertolucci, who also influenced Bellezza's work. The stylistic affinities between Bernardo Bertolucci's celebrated film *The Conformist* (1970), based on Alberto Moravia's best-selling 1947 novel of the same title, and Bellezza's poem are striking. The central persona of "Coliseum" recognizes he has become complicit in the dangerous machinations of a political system that have circumscribed his freedoms and duped him into believing that he has shared in its societal benefits, in ways similar to the dejected protagonist at the end of *The Conformist*. The narrator of "Coliseum," through an outpouring of propulsive language and relentless, filmlike tracking of images, witnesses the full extent of his own psychic and sexual dislocation, as a "vile extension" of a "damned neo-capitalist world."

Bellezza produced his most daring writing during and in the aftermath of a precarious age in Italy that witnessed the ruthless murder of his mentor and friend Pier Paolo Pasolini, among countless other anti-gay crimes.[23] Complex and emblematic sociopolitical violence of this sort was common and many of Bellezza's poems pulsate with a destabilizing fervor that interrogates disaster and impending death. Another case from the era that fueled Bellezza's outrage involved the brutal murder of RAI television executive Guido Druetto in April 1975, some six months before Pasolini's murder. In an age of oppressive social institutions and clandestine political assassinations, Druetto was also allegedly murdered by a gay liaison. Bellezza published a strong condemnation of societal indifference to this specific case that included his own manifesto-like exhortation for "HOMOSEXUALS OF THE WORLD [TO] UNITE!"—in the then-influential (now defunct) Roman newspaper *Paese Sera*.[24] One of the most notorious illustrations of the era's lawlessness and political unrest occurred a few years later in the spring of 1978, when the left-leaning president of the Democratic Christian Party, Aldo Moro, was kidnapped and brutally murdered by the Red Brigades. His bullet-riddled body was recovered behind the back seat of a car near the Communist Party Headquarters, just a short walk from Bellezza's apartment.[25]

The frequent and engaging essays Bellezza published in a variety of mainstream and lesser-known journals, magazines, and newspapers, before and after he was awarded the career-making Viareggio Prize in 1976 for his second poetry collection *Morte segreta* (*Secret Death*), helped him build a literary platform at a crucial time in Italy's sociopolitical history. As a poet of "outrage" and "scandal"—words that recur in various guises some twenty times in the poems—Bellezza was unabashed in interrogating the nuances of these concepts, from the invective-laced early poems to the "*oltraggio atomico*," or atomic disaster and ongoing psychic violation he describes in later poems.

"*La corte dei miracoli*": The Transformational Middle Years and a "*Miraculous Entourage*" of Enduring Effects

In the masterful poetry of his middle period, the omnipresent invective against societal restraint and ungrateful lovers of Bellezza's previous work becomes more intimate and formally integrated, and less mannered. The incisive and lyrical *Libro d'amore* (1981) chronicles a more sustained and poignant failed relationship in a multifaceted way full of conflicting emotion. Bellezza produced his strongest, most wide-ranging and cohesive collection, his fourth, *io* (lowercase intentional, 1983), during this middle decade of his literary production. The 1980s registers an exciting aesthetic breakthrough, as Bellezza's experiments with journaling, serial poems, and writing poetic sequences become more agile and syntactically challenging. In *io*, Bellezza explores ideas of death and impermanence, along with the enduring value of poetry and art related to a sublime and a metaphysical afterlife. Bellezza's animistic relationship to his beloved cats opens up metaphors of larger associational power, and a critique of emotional intimacy. The poems of this middle period are more spontaneous and musical, and the most intellectually ambitious. Not only does Bellezza, in keeping with Rimbaud, question the stability of the lyric "I," he also outlines a sophisticated relationship to history, myth, and fate by punning on the title of his collection. "*io*" does not only mean "me" or "I." In Italian (Spanish, French, and Portuguese, among other languages), "Io" also refers to the classical Greek-era priestess of Hera who was raped and turned into a cow by Zeus to escape Hera's jealous wrath. In astronomy, Io is also the most volcanic and unstable of Jupiter's four moons, while in Italian, *io* refers to the psychoanalytic concept of the ego and the *super-io* to the superego.

The ubiquitous cats of *io* (1983) reappear as moving leitmotifs influenced by animal spirits in later collections, and morph into mutable snake figure(s) of *Serpenta* (*Snakewoman*, 1987). Eerie animal imagery also permeates the poems of *L'avversario* (1994), from the ominous "inedible bats" of the collection's first poem to the "bird of evil omen" in the long sequence "Restless Larvae" ("Inquiete Larve") toward the end of the collection. In these transformational, Ovid-inspired re-creations beginning in the 1980s, Bellezza upends ideas about gender limits, and he explores daring figurations that call on embodiments of epic female strength while also interrogating the Edenic concept of original sin. Bellezza's language anticipates and explores a progressive discourse about queer and transgender culture some thirty years ahead of its time. While the priestess-like "transsexual" figure of his novel *Il Carnefice* (1973) from the previous decade controls key moments of that work's action, she nonetheless remains a veiled, underdeveloped persona. By contrast, in many of the poems of *Serpenta* (1987)—and especially in his novel *Turbamento* (*Disturbance*, 1984)—Bellezza foregrounds an elusive gender-nonconforming figure who charts a complex and "incantatory" path toward redemption that is neither linear nor causal. Many of the poems in *Serpenta*, dedicated to Elsa Morante, are the products of more than a fifteen-year period, and Bellezza collected them in three separate publications, which speaks to her influence and the power of their shared ideas. These poems of psychic integration that emphasize fluid transformation, together with those poems sympathetic to his literary heroes/heroines, rank among the most memorable of Bellezza's oeuvre. Bellezza's turbulent friendship with Morante, a powerful maternal figure and an impetuous mentor, would become a personal and writerly obsession, the subject of many of his poems, and significant parts of no less than four thinly veiled autobiographical novels: two written in the 1970s that reference their tempestuous bond, and two from the 1980s as Morante became ill and they drifted irrevocably apart.

In the 1980s, Bellezza's work increasingly explores a documentary, quotidian, and hyperrealistic sensibility that departs from many of his earlier influences. Bellezza's insistence on exploring complex representations of gay/queer lifestyles—cruising, prostitution, sexual abuse, multiple sex partners—and the so-called abject (a word he uses repeatedly throughout his writing) further echoes recent theories about a less condemnatory, but also oppositional or "antisocial turn" in queer studies.[26] Bellezza boldly documents the nuances of queer eroticism across varying literary genres, in a body of work of remarkably sustained achievement and intensity. By the mid-1980s, his work becomes marginalized,

Likely because of its homosexual content and the growing hysteria surrounding the AIDS epidemic. During these years, Bellezza also maintained a close friendship with Calabrian poet Dante Maffia, who helped him purchase a small house in Rocca Imperiale not far from the Ionian Sea, where Bellezza spent nearly twenty years traveling throughout southern Italy, the Mediterranean, and parts of North Africa, experiences often reflected in his work.[27]

Between the publication of *Serpenta* (*Snakewoman*, 1987) and the publication of *Libro di poesia* (*Poetry Book*, 1990), Bellezza learned definitively that he had become HIV positive, as many of the poems in the latter collection suggest. September 1990 also marked another personal crisis in Bellezza's life, as his mentor and dear friend Alberto Moravia died. During a late interview, Bellezza cheekily recounts that "even in his much-reduced old age, Moravia loved to go out to dinner with all the queers of Italy that he [Bellezza] introduced him to."[28] In this hilarious anecdote, the tone of which strikes a convincing note of casual reportage and inclusiveness, Bellezza also declares that Moravia referred to these gay friends and acquaintances as "*la corte dei miracoli*," Bellezza's "miraculous entourage" or fabulous coterie.

Libro di poesia (*Poetry Book*) registers a heightened sense of self-reckoning, while further including some of Bellezza's most powerful environmentally aware poems written in the wake of the Chernobyl nuclear disaster in the spring of 1986. *Libro di poesia* also includes a compendium of earlier poems that are explicitly more sexual and political, many of which he was reluctant or unable to publish in mainstream publications until this maturing time of his career. Bellezza's poems of the late 1980s and 1990s, as a consequence of his HIV status, no doubt, naturally assimilate metaphors of illness; they also explore the ongoing strife and mystical qualities of southern Italy to provide respite from what he perceived as the continual pretentiousness of urban literary life. His early Catholic education instilled an appreciation for religious themes of biblical exile, what critics refer to as a voice that "shouts in the desert."[29] Many of the elegiac poems of transit and metaphysical tension from the 1990s juxtapose the love of southern Italian culture with his sense of an imminent apocalyptic end of life, and the promise of an unspecified afterlife. Yet his work is never grim even under dire circumstances.

A sardonic humor consistently ensures that Bellezza's work remains fresh and never maudlin or self-pitying.

With regard to Bellezza's ever evolving and eclectic poetics, Constantine Cavafy remained a notable influence. Cavafy's often understated, conversational style and his indebtedness to classical culture is characteristic of exemplary poems such as "Gatti" ("Cats") and "Il fascino" ("Glamour"), which recalls Cavafy's famous "Ithaca." In its headlong, crescendoing rhythms and careful repetitions, "Glamour" is equally otherworldly and disarming. Thinking of God not merely as awe-inspiring but also as "glamorous" renders this one of Bellezza's most endearing poems, even as it serves comically to deflate the intensity of his well-documented suffering and battle with AIDS-related infections in a country where still today gay rights sadly lag behind. Bellezza was unable to tolerate the early stages of AZT protocols and was often mocked publicly for believing in and advocating for experimental treatments, including one expensive pseudoscientific autoimmune boosting machine that was later confiscated by public officials and proven to be ineffective.[30]

L'avversario (*The Adversary*, 1994) and the posthumously published *Proclama sul fascino* (*Proclamation on Glamour*, 1996) chart new territories where Bellezza's voice becomes more prayerful and resigned, though no less polemical in the face of an indifferent Italian society that was also confronting consistent government corruption and pernicious mafia violence. Much of Bellezza's language in these two later collections draws flatly from the common juridical and political parlance of the era, where especially in Sicily, *Cosa Nostra* led a full-scale "Second War" that famously witnessed the bombing death in 1992 of influential anti-mafia magistrates Giovanni Falcone and Paolo Borsellino. Other mafia terrorism of the era occurred throughout Italian cities and tourist destinations in Florence, Milan, and Rome, among others. The title of Bellezza's last collection can be read as a pun on the frequent, ponderous *proclami* or "proclamations" that many accused *mafiosi* would read during court trials.[31]

Not all of Bellezza's poems easily cohere—their sum at times can seem greater than individual poems' occasionally jarring parts. That may well be the point, as he challenges readers to be more aesthetically ambitious and far-reaching, and to begin a reconsideration of the work as part of an interconnected whole. Bellezza's poetry consistently strikes a cultural nerve as it speaks frankly about sexuality, mortality, and issues of an emerging queer identity without pandering or being reductively political. Poet Maurizio Cucchi has highlighted Bellezza's "ecstasy of the quotidian," which seems related to his heightened goals of documenting queer subjectivity while also linking a sense of universal alienation with a poetics that unites postmodern playfulness, archaism, and direct speech.[32] The relentless demands of his art, of writing compelling and strikingly probing poems, were foremost on Bellezza's mind throughout his writing life. While his work is frequently direct and unsettling, it is also consistently exhilarating and visionary. The work is by turns often tender and resigned, especially in the mid-career and late poems where he grapples to understand his loss of romantic desire and to accept his AIDS diagnosis in a culture of limited tolerance. The sheer variety of forms, from epigram to bold love-lyric to sustained political narrative, coupled with the intensity and insistence of Bellezza's voice, make a compelling argument for his lasting importance among the best poets of the second half of the twentieth century.

Notes

1. Enzo Siciliano, "Amor di poeti," *La Stampa* 105, no. 151 (July 2, 1971), Rome: Archivio Centrale dello Stato, Consoli Archive, Binder 294, http://www.archiv iolastampa.it/. "Scava più in là dell'inerzia vitale dove la mortalità prende a balbettare, il suo credo." All translations from the Italian are mine unless otherwise noted.

2. On November 2, 1975, Pasolini was brutally beaten, then run over, allegedly by a gang of gay pick-ups, because of his leftist politics. Bellezza wrote two well-known, book-length nonfictional meditations on the murder: Dario Bellezza, *Morte di Pasolini* (Milan: Mondadori, 1981); and Dario Bellezza, *Il poeta assassinato: Una riflessione, un'ipotesi, una sfida sulla morte di Pier Paolo Pasolini* (Venice: Gli specchi Marsilio, 1996). For a more thorough accounting of the crime, see Simona Zecchi, *Pasolini, massacro di un poeta* (Milan: Adriano Salani Editore, 2015).

3. Enzo Paris, "Dario Bellezza, il poeta maudit," *Il manifesto*, March 30, 2021, https://ilmanifesto.it/dario-bellezza-il-poeta-maudit, cites Carmen Giardina and Massimiliano Palmese's *Bellezza addio* (Rome: Zhivago, Luce Cinecitta, 2023); and a biographical novel by Igor Patruno that is also underway. See also

the excellent interview by Marta Rizzo, "Bellezza addio: Lo scandalo come responsabilità. Intervista a Carmen Giardina," *Articolo 21*, February 17, 2024, https://www.articolo21.org/2024/02/bellezza-addio-lo-scandalo-come-respon sabilita-intervista-a-carmen-giardina/.

4. Maurizio Gregorini, *Morte di Bellezza, storia di una verità nascosta* (Rome: Castelvecchi, 1997), 58, 67.

5. Laura Ruberto and Joseph Sciorra, eds., introduction to *New Italian Migration to the United States*, vol. 1 (Urbana: University of Illinois Press, 2017),
6. The number quoted here is approximately 28.5 million, more than 14 million of whom immigrated to the United States.

6. Cristina Lombardi-Diop and Caterina Romeo, "Introduction: Paradigms of Postcoloniality in Contemporary Italy," in *Postcolonial Italy: Challenging National Homogeneity* (New York: Palgrave Macmillan, 2012), 5–9. Lombardi-Diop and Romeo expand Antonio Gramsci's idea of subalternity on the Southern Question by arguing that "migration flows to industrialized regions of the North of Italy from the South" render southern Italians as "colonial migrants" who experience much of the psychic displacement and are "routinely discrimi-nated against as second-class citizens in the labor and housing market."

7. Bassani was part of the jury, which included Maria Luisa Spaziani, Attilio Bertolucci, and Mario Luzi, among others, who awarded Bellezza the Montale Prize in 1994. Quoted in Velio Carratoni, "Omaggio a Dario Bellezza, Premio Montale 1994, XII edizione, Relazione finale," *Fermenti*, no. 209 (1994): 118, Con-soli Archive, Binder 295.

8. On the back cover of Bellezza's first collection, *Invettive e licenze* (Milan: Garzanti, 1971), Pasolini would herald him as "the best poet of a new genera-tion." See also Bellezza, *Il poeta assassinato*, 80: "il mio segretariato, che più che segretariato era stato un corso accelerato di poesia, una palestra di poesia." Maurizio Gegorini, in *Il male di Dario Bellezza* (Viterbo: Nuovi Equilibri, 2006), 20, reports that Bellezza served as Pasolini's secretary from 1966 to 1969.

9. Myriam Cristallo, *Uscir Fuori, Dieci anni di lotte omosessuali in Italia; 1971–1981* (Rome: Sandro Teti editore, 2017), 52–55. Writing in the mid-1990s, Cris-tallo, in her otherwise excellent text, anachronistically lambastes Bellezza's novel *Lettere da Sodoma* (Milan: Garzanti, 1972), the first major commercially success-ful gay-themed novel written by a self-declared gay man. Many news clippings and other personal effects from the Consoli archive tell a much more nuanced story about the tensions between the FUORI! gay rights movement that orig-inated in Turin and included Cristallo, and its counterpart in Rome. Bellezza was reluctant to support organized political causes and was critical of the Com-munist Party and the Radical Party's subsequent affiliation with FUORI! For early examples of Bellezza's activism, see D. Bellezza, "La condizione di quelli

che sono diversi," *Paese Sera* September 15, 1972, Consoli Archive, Binder 294; and Bellezza, "Un mondo senza poesia, Gli Occhi *di Pino Pelosi,*" *Paese Sera,* May 4, 1976, Consoli Archive, Binder 294.

10. Adele Cambria, "I buoni consigli," in *Addio amori, addio cuori: Dario Bellezza,* ed. Antonio Veneziani (Rome: Fermenti, 1996), 81.

11. Biancamaria Frabotta, "A Dario Bellezza, tentato di risorgere," in *L'arcano fascino dell'amore tradito,* ed. Fabrizio Cavallaro (Rome: Giulio Perrone Editore, 2006), 50; Jennifer Scappettone, ed. and trans., *Locomotrix: Selected Poetry and Prose of Amelia Rosselli* (Chicago: University of Chicago Press, 2012), 14, 15. Scappettone asserts that Rosselli's idea of the "lapsus" is more concerned with "linguistic invention" than a "purely Freudian mnemonic forgetting." Bellezza also shares Rosselli's interest in what Scappettone emphasizes as "baroque or absurd turns of phrase or syllables in use in Italy specially in the South [. . . and its dialects]."

12. Allen Ginsberg, letter to Dario Bellezza, February 13, 1996, Consoli Archive, Binder 297. Ginsberg writes, "Poet Dario Bellezza is a significant cultural figure. I strongly urge the Italian government to acknowledge his contribution and to afford him a stipend to make his final days more bearable." Other letters of support are in the same Binder 297. For other literary influences, see "Gatti," in this collection; and "Congedo," in *Dario Bellezza, Tutte le poesie,* ed. Roberto Deidier (Rome: Mondadori, 2015), 544. Other key literary forebears or "major teacher figures" to whom Bellezza alludes specifically include Pasolini, Ginsberg, Cavafy, Leopardi, Baudelaire, Morante, Rimbaud, and Bataille.

13. Peter Covino, "Dario Bellezza, Biographical Notes," *Atlanta Review* 27, no. 2 (2011): 174.

14. See Keith Harvey, "Translating Camp Talk: Gay Identities and Cultural Transfer," in *The Translations Studies Reader,* 2nd ed., ed. Lawrence Venuti (London: Routledge, 2004), 408; and Stephen Orgel, "Ganymede Agonistes," *GLQ: A Journal of Lesbian and Gay Studies* 12, no. 3 (2004): 485–501, for Orphic iconography during the Renaissance and classical models of man-youth ephebic sexuality.

15. Gualtiero De Santi, "Nel cerchi della modernità," in Veneziani, *Addio amori, addio cuori,* 7. In the same volume, Giorgio Manacorda, "Versi spudorati," is especially complex when he says "La poesie di Bellezza si distingue perché sceglie con decisione il discorso letterario eccessivo, teatrale" (Bellezza's poetry distinguishes itself because it definitively chooses an excessive and theatrical literary discourse [23]). See also, in *Addio amori,* Plinio Perelli, "Poeta puro, poeta nato," 48–49; and Enzo Siciliano, "La busta gialla," 97.

16. Andrea Zanzotto, "Ritmi e cadenze solo sue," in Veneziani, *Addio amori, addio cuori,* 131, describes Bellezza's poetic prose as "ricca di una infuocata tensione."

17. Massimo Consoli, *Affetti Speciali* (Bolsena: Massari editore, 1999), 202–5, includes pertinent facts quoted in this paragraph. See also Massimo Consoli, C.I.D.A.M.S. letter, from Massimo Consoli to Dario Bellezza, Centro Italiano per la Documentazione delle Attività delle Minoranze Sociali (Italian Center for the Documentation of Social Minorities) Archive, Binder 294, Corrispondenza, Istituto Italiano di Storia Sociale, January 2, 1974. See also Angela Azzaro, "Da Stonewall al Colosseo," *Liberazione*, September 8, 2000, IV, V. In honor of International Gay Pride, Rome 2000, Consoli Archive, Binder 295.

18. Untitled publicity flyer located in the Consoli Archive, Binder 294 (1973–78). See also Consoli's letter, "La Gay House Chiusa dal Comune," *Corriere della Sera*, January 2, 1981, Binder 295.

19. Sharon Wood and Joseph Farrell, "Other Voices Contesting the Status Quo," in *The Cambridge Companion to Modern Italian Culture*, ed. Zygmunt Baranski and Rebecca J. West (Cambridge: Cambridge University Press, 2001), 137. For a longer list of terrorism and social events that affected poets of the era, see Maria Borio, *Poetiche e individui: La poesia italiana dal 1970 al 2000* (Venice: Marsilio, 2018), 22.

20. The Castleporziano Literary Festival was held June 28–30, 1979, near Ostia, where Pasolini was murdered. Footage of the event, which on the first night descended into mayhem with spectators as Bellezza was reading, is available in Andrea Anderman's documentary film *Castelporziano Ostia dei Poeti* (1981), also available at the Allen Ginsberg Project, accessed February 29, 2024, https://allenginsberg.org/2012/08/castelporziano/. See the link to LeRoi Jones reading and a sung poem by Allen Ginsberg. See also Gianluca Rizzo, *Poetry on the Stage: The Theatre of the Italian Avant-Garde* (Toronto: University of Toronto Press, 2020), 211–18. Rizzo's impressive scholarship and lively critique of the theater scene of the era, in which Bellezza also participated peripherally, provide a comprehensive overview.

21. Vicenzo Salsetta, "*Il dio che non c'è*," in Cavallaro, *L'arcano fascino*, 76. For Beat Generation influences and an assessment of Bellezza's performance style at Castelporziano, see also Borio, *Poetiche individui*, 48, 49.

22. Quoted in Gregorini, "Colloquio col poeta," in *Morte di Bellezza*, 46–48.

23. Cristallo, *Uscir Fuori*, 135–36. For continued discussion of violent crime in a known cruising area, see also Susanna Nirenstein, "Gay a Monte Caprino: 'È ora di finirla,' Dario Bellezza parla, dei recenti episodi di violenza," *La Repubblica*, September 30, 1984.

24. Dario Bellezza, "La penultima pagina Ompo" April 1, 1975, ed. Massimo Consoli, accessed January 24, 2019, http://www.culturagay.it/documento/29. At the end of this article, Bellezza avers that readers "must reawaken their consciousness and scream their queerness to the world" (*Risvegliatevi alla coscienza*,

gridate al mondo la vostra diversità, OMOSESSUALI DI TUTTO IL MONDO, UNITEVI!). See also D. Bellezza, "La condizione di quelli che sono diversi," *Paese Sera,* September 15, 1972, Consoli Archive, Binder 294; and Bellezza, "Un mondo senza poesia, Gli Occhi *di Pino Pelosi,*" *Paese Sera,* May 4, 1976, Consoli Archive, Binder 294.

25. Henry Tanner, "Moro Slain, Body Found in Rome," *New York Times,* May 10, 1978.

26. Donald E. Hall and Annamarie Jagose, eds., *The Routledge Queer Studies Reader* (Abingdon: Routledge, 2013), xv–xvi. Hall and Jagose contend that their *Queer Studies Reader* builds on ideas from the *Lesbian and Gay Studies Reader* (New York: Routledge, 1993), which was also a "site of inquiry into many forms of sexual non-conformity, including for instance, bisexuality, trans-sexualism, and sadomasochism." See also Leo Bersani, "Is the Rectum a Grave?," *October* 43 (Winter 1987): 197–222. Bersani eschews moralism and builds on ideas of radical sexual pluralism by insisting on "the diversity of human sexuality in all its variant forms as perhaps the most radical part of gay culture" (218, 219).

27. Dante Maffia, "Ricordo di Dario Bellezza," in Cavallaro, *L'arcano fascino,* 53. See also Gregorini, *Morte di Bellezza,* 57; Mario Revelli, "Incontro in Basilicata con Dario Bellezza, Se scrivessi canzonette e non poesie," *La Gazzetta del Mezzogiorno,* January 17, 1980, Consoli Archive, Binder 295. Bellezza speaks of his love for Magna Grecia (*sic*), his mother's roots in Taranto, and his thoughts on the oil crisis and the dangers of nuclear proliferation.

28. Gregorini, *Morte di Bellezza,* 49: "Io gli ho presentato tutti i froci d'Italia e lui è stato molto signore a subirseli tutti. Diceva infatti che quando si usciva con me si usciva con la corte dei miracoli." In fact, Bellezza uses the more aggressive term *froci.* Cavallaro, *L'arcano fascino,* 8. Both mention "corte dei miracoli," which is also a fictional locale referenced in Carlo Collodi's famous *Pinocchio.*

29. Gabriella Sica, "Dario Bellezza, voce di uno che grida nel deserto," in Cavallaro, *L'arcano fascino,* 100.

30. Gregorini, *Morte di Bellezza,* 74–75, 105–6, 110.

31. Francesco La Licata, *Storia di Giovanni Falcone,* 5th ed. (Milan: Mondadori, Universal Economica, 2006), 43–44.

32. Dario Bellezza, *Proclama sul fascino* (Milan: Mondadori, 1996), back cover; A. Veneziani, *Addio amori, addio cuori,* 22; see also Gualtiero di Santi, "All'origine della poesia di Bellezza," in Cavallaro, *L'arcano fascino,* 28–38.

WHAT SEX IS DEATH?

Invettive e licenze (1971)

Invective and License

QUALE SESSO HA LA MORTE?

Con quale sesso mi verrai incontro,
se Orfeo scalmanato non mi riguarda
e Euridice era un troia infingarda?

Addio scemenza mia trangugiata
in tutta fretta dentro una fratta,
il sapore si perde nella notte dei delinquenti
che ricattano la loro semenza con gli schiaffi
della certezza, al cinema di periferia.

Ma quale sesso ha la morte?
È ragazzo. È ragazza. Spaventosamente
materna mi abbraccia al limitare del sonno,
quando l'alba affretta la suo agonia
e il giorno calza i suoi colori di malinconia;
quando l'orina preme nella vescica
e il sesso prega le sue erezioni di non fare
troppo male, di non troppo eccitare il compagno
tacito e notturno;
l'occhiuto grembo rimane ad ascoltare allora
il mio bisogno di preghiera detta ad alta voce:
"Signore, illeso il giudizio aspetto, la mia morte.
Non l'aspetto che come giustiziera, avvocato
del diavolo, in un curialesco ufficio celimontano.
In terra certa sprofondami. Che io non debba
patire in mia morte la mia sopravvivenza.

Signore, fammi morire tutto, eternamente.
I morti non mi abbiano loro sodale spento.
È lontano il giorno della mia creazione.
È vicino il giorno della mia distruzione".

WHAT SEX IS DEATH?

With what sex will you meet me,
if hotheaded Orpheus ignores me
and Eurydice was an idle streetwalker?

Goodbye to my quickly gulped down
stupidity among the thickets,
its taste is lost in the night where delinquents
extort their seed with slaps
of assurance, at a suburban theater.

But what sex is death?
Boy. Girl. Terrifyingly
maternal, it embraces me to limit sleep,
when dawn hastens its agony
and day displays its melancholy hues;
when urine presses against the bladder
and its sex begs erections not to hurt
too much, not to excite the silent
nocturnal friend;
the many-eyed womb waits to listen then
to my need for out loud prayer:
"Lord, unscathed I await judgment, my death
I await solely as executioner, advocate
of the devil, in a lawyer's office of Celimontano.
Plunge me into solid ground. So that
in death I won't be grieved by my survival.

Lord, let all of me die, eternally.
The dead count me among close friends.
The day of my creation is far away.
The day of my destruction near."

Infante di una infanzia un po' cresciuta
tu dovevi sollevare il mondo senza i miei
muscoli d'oro e seguirmi nell'Inferno
casto dei miei piaceri proibiti, non
mutarti mai in angelo ma bestia rimanere
alle mie morte dimostrazioni razionali:

squisito e losco servitore nella serra
dell'alchimista a rovescio che l'oro
dell'ambizione trasforma in vile
metallo, senza ricevere compenso
per il suo servile facchinaggio.

Per te le finte parole del finto poeta che ero:
al minuto la minutaglia rivendevo
sul mercato libertino delle fratte
o dei monumenti male illuminati:

assassinato ingegno insaccato
di stolte immagini cullate dalla
Follia e dal Fato fino all'oscenità.

Per il tuo calore di caino bambino
che non perdona la maldicenza
di essere nato senza il companatico
del sesso e del peccato.

Se dare gratis quel che gratis
abbiamo ricevuto è solo dare
a rate l'odore della memoria
a comodo comodamente rivisitata
allora in verità se uno mi dice:
"Dio del sesso rotto a tutti i corpi"
è la puzza del mio alito a tradirmi!

Infant of a slightly precocious infancy
you were supposed to lift up the world without
my golden muscles and follow me into Hell
chastened from my forbidden desires, don't
ever turn into an angel but remain a beast
toward my deadening rational displays:

exquisite and corrupt servant in the laboratory
of the backward alchemist who transforms
the gold of ambition into a vile
metal, without compensation
for his servile drudgery.

For you the feigned words from the fake poet I was:
by the minute I resold the minutiae
on the libertine market of the shrubbery
or of the poorly illumined monuments:

murdered genius overburdened
with simpleminded images culled from
Folly and Fate all the way to obscenity.

For your Cain-like and childish ire
that doesn't forgive the curse
of being born without the bread and butter
of sex and sin.

If to give away freely what we freely
received is merely to layaway
the scent of revisited memory
as a loan comfortably repaid
then in truth if someone calls me a:
"God of the broken sex of all bodies,"
it's the smell of my breath that betrays me!

L'insonnia che mi prende
la mattina scompare.

Ma più difficile è cercarti
così ridotto, in malora
dentro la nostra tana.

Stanza che descrivo assolata:
il largo letto matrimoniale,
l'odore del mio corpo
e non il tuo.

The insomnia that grips me
disappears in the morning.

Yet it's more difficult to look for you
so diminished, in the ruin
of our cage.

Room I describe as sun-drenched:
the large double bed,
the scent of my body
and not yours.

Ascoltavo la morte nel mio sogno
di pazzo dirmi all'orecchio soave:
"Ti trascuro. No verrò mai da te."

Allora mi ricordai di te e mi svegliai.
La morte mi era a lato. La notte
riempiva la stanza di silenzio.
Alla finestra la luce della luna. E

nel mio cuore un presentimento.

I listened to death in my dream
of madness tell me softly in my ear:
"I'm neglecting you. I will never come to you."

Then I remembered you and I awoke.
Death was by my side. The night
filled the room with silence.
At the window the glow of the moon. And

in my heart a presentiment.

A Elsa Morante

I ragazzi drogati, guardie del corpo
dell'Assoluto, vanno per il mondo
mattutino fino alla sera della loro
sopravvivenza: come passerotti
mangiano distrattamente
tutti presi dai loro sogni d'avventura.

È la sciagura che li coglie per strada
e li fulmina piamente stecchiti
li lascia prede delle iene umane
che scrivono i loro necrologi sui giornali.

Le loro dita sono piene di anelli,
la loro grazia bugiarda di mentire
sa che io non ho bisogno di droghe.

E mi guardano come un povero reietto,
un infelice, ma troppo non m'offendo.
So che vanno per le vie del mondo
con in bocca il sapore della polvere
e del tossico:
strepito vano è il loro baloccarsi
bambino, orgoglio luciferino
di chi si consuma, strugge come cera,
ma anche così la mia voce smorta
li vorrà sempre al mio capezzale.

To Elsa Morante

The drug addicts, bodyguards
of the Absolute, roam the earth
from morning until the night of
their final survival: like sparrows
they eat distractedly
seized by their dreams of adventure.

And the disaster that gathers them in the street
and devoutly strikes them stone-cold
leaves them prey to human hyenas
who write their obituaries in the papers.

Their fingers are full of rings;
their graceful, fallacious way of lying
knows I have no need of drugs.

And they look at me like a poor outcast
unfortunate one, but I'm not too offended.
I know they roam the streets of the world
with mouths tasting of dust
and poison:
their puerile play
is vain chaos, diabolical pride
of they who consume themselves, burn waxlike,
but even then my faint song
always summons them to my bedside.

A Pier Paolo Pasolini

M'aggiro fra ricatti e botte e licenzio
la mia anima mezza vuota e peccatrice

e la derelitta crocifissione mia sola
sa chi sono: spia e ricattatore
che odia i suoi simili. E non trovo

pace in questa sordida lotta
contro la mia rovina, il suo sfacelo.

Dio! Non attendo che la morte.
Ignoro il corso della Storia. So solo
la bestia che è in me e latra.

To Pier Paolo Pasolini

I'm surrounded by blackmail and beatings
and I dismiss my half-empty and sinful soul

and only my own derelict crucifixion
knows who I am: spy and blackmailer
who hates those of like mind. I find

no peace in this sordid battle
against my own ruins, this debacle.

God! I expect nothing but death.
I ignore the course of History. I know
only the beast within who howls.

Se viene la guerra
non partirò soldato.

Ma di nuovo gli usati treni
porteranno i giovani soldati
lontano a morire dalle madri.

Se viene la guerra
non partirò soldato.

Sarò traditore
della vana patria.

Mi farò fucilare
come disertore.

        Mia nonna, da ragazzino
        mi raccontava:
        "Tu non eri ancora nato. Tua madre
        ti aspettava. Io già pensavo
        dentro il rifugio osceno
        ma caldo di tanti corpi, gli uni
        agli altri stretti, come tanti
        apparenti fratelli, alle favole
        che avrebbero portato il sonno
        a te, che, Dio non voglia!,
        non veda più guerra".

If there's a war
I won't enlist.

Yet once again rickety trains
bring young soldiers
faraway from their mothers to die.

If there's a war
I won't enlist.

I ll be a traitor
of this useless country.

And get shot
as a deserter.

> When I was child, my grandmother
> used to recount:
> "You weren't born yet. Your mother
> was expecting you. I was already thinking
> in that hot obscene refuge
> of so many bodies, each
> clutching one another, seemingly
> like brothers, about fairytales
> which would make you sleepy,
> and that, God willing!, you'd
> see no more wars."

ALL'AMBRA JOVINELLI

I

Cinema in penombra che m'accoglievi
pomeridiano ragazzo imberbe
col pudore infedele e rauco alla bisogna
taciturna dell'amore desolato,
m'accogli e m'adagi su una tua
cigolante poltrona. Vuoto d'intorno
lo scenario dei miei teatrati lutti
aspetta di riempirsi tacitamente
servile, di sorde complicità fasciato,
di labbra sottili che vanno e vengono
di nervose mani che cercano altre mani:
simmetrie d'emisferi rapidamente penetrati.

II

L'errore qui non esiste. Esistono
infelici gli errori di un attimo
che piamente il destino s'affanna
ad inseguire nel lurido gabinetto,
dove ogni regola è un labirinto
che conduce al Minotauro feroce
e i giorni preparati della morte
sono concessi alla vita fisiologica:
coltello per uccidere il mio cuore
dove cade il Tempo di vivermi
così prontamente:
labirinto che non conduce a nessuna
salute del piacere e dell'eccesso
non ha che la sua fine nel sesso,
ma è il tempo solo che vola
senza senso, nel riflesso di questo
trapasso arcaico ai ginnasi d'Atene.

At the Amber Palace

I

Dim-lit theater that welcomed me
on afternoons as a smooth-faced boy
with a hoarse and shameless need for
wordless desolate love,
you welcome me and ease me onto
your squeaky seat. Hollow within
this scene of theatrical grief
that awaits its tacit servile
fulfillment, bound, deaf, and complicit,
to tight lips that come and go
to nervous hands that search for other hands:
symmetries of quickly penetrated meridians.

II

Error doesn't exist here. Unhappily
errors of the moment exist
that destiny piously hurries along
to chase into the lurid bathroom,
where every rule is a labyrinth
that leads to the ferocious Minotaur
and the days readied by death
are conceded to a physiological existence:
knife to stake my heart
where the Time to live my life wanes
too readily:
labyrinth that doesn't lead to any
healthy pleasure or excess
there's no end except in sex,
but it's only time that vacillates
without sense, in the reflection of this
archaic passage to Athenian gymnasiums.

III

Urlo qui la mia fame, un gesto
ripeto quotidiano, cercato
e ritrovato in trecento lirette
confuse nelle sacche sporche
di innamorati palpeggiamenti.

IV

Addio adolescenza, miserabili catene
della speranza! Ora è lividamente certa
all'eccitato una mano presta
a piegarlo al furtivo amore
del povero: strapazzo breve,
fracasso di poltrona addomesticata
da qualche sudore di ragazzetto
che sognando di . . . nel sesso ingordo
della sua ragazza, aspetta docile
il cliente, la richiesta infame
di chi guardando la vita addormentato
crudelmente è risvegliato alla realtà
dalla mobile vita che si muove
dentro i calzoni di qualche ragazzo.

V

Fuori i ragazzi andranno lieti in giro.
Scenderanno a fiume a raccogliere
i frutti di qualche loro segreto:
maschile presenza dell'inconscio
ambivalente che sgomina il giorno
femminile e austero di sapersi fonte
di lucro, pieno di morte da congedare
virilmente.

III

Here I howl my hunger, a repeated
daily gesture, sought
and found in three hundred mishandled
lire in the grubby pockets
of groping lovers.

IV

Goodbye adolescence, miserable chains
of faith! It's bruisingly certain now
a hand will press the aroused
bending him to the sordid love
of a pathetic man: cheap thrill,
of a creaky seat tamed
by some kid's sweat who's
fantasizing about . . . .the eager sex
of his girlfriend, obediently waiting
the client's vile request
of he who sleepwalks through life
crudely reawakened to reality
by the fitful shifting
in some boy's pants.

V

Outside the boys go about happily.
Down to the river to reap
the fruits of their secret:
manly figure of divided
consciousness that dismantles daylight
with a woman's sober acceptance
of financial gain, and a dead
virility to expend.

VI

Io, con gli occhi bendati, assente,
sbandito uccello della notte
perso in un inutile richiamo
batto nel freddo i piedi
e la mia storia solo da me saputa
si perde chiara nella lieve nebbia
del fiume che arresta il mio cuore
ad un sogno illuso, presente
come Dio ovunque impaziente
si apra all'aria un sesso di ragazzetto,
e qui, lontananza infallibile,
affanno cieco, coi ragazzi
a lato che la pubertà infiora
sul volto amato di miseria,
il tempo si dilata, finalmente esiste
nel possesso dell'occhio che trascura il film
e l'impossibile come fulmine precipita.

VII

Ma è notte ormai per il poeta
che al falso abbraccio della modernità
preferisce la grande stella del tramonto della civiltà.
Irsuta stella in corsa ancora
ma quasi tramontata ormai
che non si moltiplica più
in migliaia di stelle lontane.
Ogni alba è una resurrezione, ritorno
alla pluralità, ma noi abitatori della notte
non arriveremo mai all'amore
della nostra decadenza!
Cancellando il nome dell'amore
dal Libro della vita, ci si ritrova
qui a spetalare un sesso . . .
come fosse la fine del mondo.

VI

Blindfolded, dazed,
Like a banished nightingale,
I'm lost in a cautionary tale
slogging through the cold
my plight known only to me
is fading in the dim fog
of the river that stops my heart
at a deluded dream, present
as if God everywhere impatient
were opening up a boy's sex to the air,
and here, in the surefire distance,
breathless and blind, with boys
by my side whose cherished
miserable faces bloom in puberty,
time expands, and finally exists
in the knowledge of the eye that ignores the film
and the impossible strikes like lightning.

VII

But it's nighttime already for the poet
who at the false embrace of modernity
prefers the great star at the sunset of civilization.
Fuzzy star still in orbit
but almost faded by now
that no longer multiplies
into thousands of faraway stars.
Every dawn is a resurrection, a return
to the multitudes, but we denizens of the night
never arrive at the love
of our own decadence!
Erasing the name of love
from the Book of life, we meet again
here to deflower sex
as if it were the end of the world.

Ti cadono i capelli, qualcuno
ti mangia il cuore. Non sai
più scrivere. Parole senza senso
immagini fiacche e vuote.

Il sole nero della morte brilla
lontano e tu t'avvicini a lui
col tuo cranio spappolato.

Anch'io ho paura. La serale
notturna mattutina insonnia
non s'affloscia: la fessura
per arrivare all'anima
è troppo volgare.

Addio. Tradiscimi con chi
ti pare.

Your hair falls out, someone
eats your heart. You no longer know
how to write. Words without meaning
wearied and empty images.

The black sun of death explodes
faraway and you get close to him
with your pulverized skull.

I too am afraid. The never-ending
nightly and early-morning insomnia
never flags: the fissure
that leads to the soul
is too vulgar.

Goodbye. Betray me
with whomever you'd like.

Morte segreta (1976)

Secret Death

E abbandono morte. Giocattolo di Dio.
Le muse se sveltiscono solo se andate cose
rigirano, sezionando in dolore e confessione,
oscillando fra tenere immagini e pensiero
lucido di ieri friabile, rendendo la memoria
delle realtà impossibili, quelle mai volute
e tutte assoldate al vizio del ricordo.
Le trapassate entità ingiuste e invivibili
che fecero di me un ragazzo come tanti e ora
un morto che cammina, un fiato eterno di pietà
e tristezza, trascinandomi un corpo-cadavere
che di mattina alzo e vesto, rantolo per casa,
chiudo al gabinetto, ascolto nelle sue chiacchiere
insulse e quotidiane, chiedendo udienza alle muse
ancora con ironia come una pianta secca
dai fiori profumati, chissà perché. Dentro
il cuore si agita invano la parola chiave, morte,
morte terrena, morte eterna, ed è il corpo trionfante
bestia che si accalda a dimostrarlo in attesa
di diventare freddo come un marmo.
Questo corpo che vesto e nutro e lavo
e accordo ai separati corpi altrui, costringo ad amare,
manometto, chiedo il perdono della sua putrefazione
perenne in una erezione instabile e impotente, sterile,
senza figli severi e solari per confortare vecchiaia.
Tutto questo decomposto, gracile corpo cadavere
devo affaticarlo per sbiancare una notte senza insonnia
uncinato da pasticche velenose; cuori diabolici nel letto
agitano la loro bandiera nevrotica. "Anche tu sei dei nostri
caro, scegli l'orgasmo che vuoi. Ti aspettiamo impazienti,
addio!" I morti, gli strabilianti morti vivendo nei sogni
li terrorizzano fino al delirio della più enorme insonnia
e solo le botte dell'infanzia mi placano, giacendo

And I abandon death. Plaything of God.
The muses hurry along only if what's gone
returns, separated into pain and confession,
oscillating between tender images and yesterday's
lucid thought crumbling, rendering the memory
of impossible realities, those never wanted
and all enlisted to the vice of remembrance.
Those unjust and unlivable past entities
that made me a boy like so many others and now
a dead man walking, an eternal breath of pity
and sorrow, dragging my cadaver-body
mornings that I wake and dress, wheeze around the house,
lock in the bathroom, while listening to his chatter
of insults and daily routines, asking the muses
for counsel ironically, like a desiccated plant
somehow still fragrant of flowers. Within
the heart that key word stirs in vain, death,
earthly death, eternal death, and it's the body triumphant
beast that sweats as proof while waiting
to become cold as a slab of marble.
This corpse I dress and feed and wash
and reconcile with other corpses, I'm forced to love,
I manhandle it and ask forgiveness of its perennial
putrefaction with a limp and impotent erection, sterile,
with neither severe nor cheerful children to comfort old age.
This entire decomposed, frail body cadaver
I need to tire out to brighten a night without insomnia
whetted by toxic pills; diabolical hearts wave
their neurotic flag in bed. "You too are one of us, dear,
choose the orgasm you want. We'll wait impatiently,
farewell!" The dead, the astounding dead living in dreams
terrorize them until the delirium of the most excessive
insomnia and the bruises of childhood placate me, lying

senza vita lontano dal centro della mia vita.
"Non urlare, Dario, non urlare, sei pazzo.
Un vivente melodramma da strapazzo!"
Così diviso da me, osservo il mio cadavere,
ne contemplo le mille epoche sopravvissute
alle illusioni, alla felicità passeggera di un bacio,
preda di sapienti ladroni notturni che sanno
aspettare fino all'ultimo l'estremo rantolo.

lifeless far from the center of my life.
"Don't yell, Dario, don't yell, you're crazy.
A living melodrama of lunacy!"
Divided from myself, I watch my cadaver,
I think about the thousand epochs it's survived
about the illusions, the fleeting happiness of a kiss,
prey of wise nocturnal thieves who understand
how to wait until that ultimate extreme gasp.

AD ANNA MARIA ORTESE

Ritorna primavera, e con essa ritorna gioventù;
il gusto alla vita ritorna che l'inverno rese
insapore e fondo di malinconia e pietà per i vivi
ritornati ad uscire dall'abisso scontento del gelo
di gennaio o del marzo piovoso. Ora che si riesce
viene naturale rievocare i vecchi tempi, alteri
e sfrontati, della giovinezza sparita fra gli
insulti e i sospiri. Riaprire le porte all'avventura
dopo i mesi di febbre e di castigo, nello spazio
di memoria amaro e sconsolato. Ma ritornato
ancora una volta nella casa-inferno-tugurio
e ancella del peccato, di non peccare audace
irresoluto peccatore, ho aperto al vento
le finestre, all'aprile incostante cercando
di succhiare una nuova linfa vitale
che mi facesse chiudere nel cassetto
dei ricordi le vecchie impressioni di morte
e spavento luttuoso fino a dormire lasciando
nel sonno ogni pensiero, senza alimento
per un futuro vuoto, libero finalmente da parole.

To Anna Maria Ortese

Spring returns, and with it youth returns;
a taste for life returns that winter rendered
tasteless and full of gloom and pity for the living
who reemerge from the cheerless abyss of January
ice or rainy March. Now that we can
it's natural to conjure up old times, haughty
and brash, from a youthfulness lost among
insults and sighs. Unbolt the doors to adventure
after months of fever and punishment, in the space
of bitter and desolate memory. But returned
again to this infernal-hovel and handmaiden
of sin, in order not to transgress bold
wavering sinner, I've opened the windows
to the wind, to fickle April trying
to savor vital new lifeblood
that would enable me to shut age-old feelings
of death and dreaded fear into a drawer
of memories until I can go to bed leaving
every thought to sleep, without sustenance
for an empty future, free at last from words.

Ho paura. Lo ripeto a me stesso
invano. Questa non è poesie né testamento.
Ho paura di morire. Di fronte a questo
che vale cercare le parole per dirlo
meglio. La paura resta, lo stesso.

Ho paura. Paura di morire. Paura
di non scriverlo perché dopo, il dopo
è più orrendo e instabile del resto.
Dover prendere atto di questo:
che si è un corpo e si muore.

I'm afraid. I repeat it to myself
in vain. This isn't poetry or testament.
I'm afraid of dying. Compared to this
what's the value of looking for words to say it
better. Fear persists, nonetheless.

I'm afraid. Afraid of dying. Afraid
of not writing it down because afterward, the after
is more horrendous and unstable than what remains.
We should all take note of this:
that we are flesh and we die.

L.S.D.

Sospiravi attendendo che facesse
la sua tossica azione. Te ne stavi

stupito di tanto languore in qualche
sole di solo drogato. La luce nel tuo volto
che io scrutavo e contavo le rughe
che segnavano il tradimento:
le occhiaie della mia perdizione.

O ragazzo, caro ragazzo andiamo
via in questo treno di aria
dalla civiltà che ci bara; accogliamo
devoti il selvaggio servaggio che è in noi,

nella notte è il silenzio che ci vince
e ci bacia e se tu rimani freddo
è allora colpa mia, della mia bocca
che non ti bacia e non riscalda
le tue labbra di bracia.

Ma guarda, ragazzo mio: la sera
ha tutto in se ravvoltolato. L'angoscia
è perfetta e nessun'altra può scuoterla
o spossessarla.

Pensa che io ti sono madre e i piccoli
fratelli sono tanti piccoli uccelli
col gozzo pieno di cibo e io sono loro
fratello e la Stazione il Pincio o il Colosseo

non ci riguardano più.

LSD

You were sighing waiting for
its toxic effects to begin. Standing there

stunned by such listlessness in some
sun only for drug addicts. I studied the light
on your face and counted the wrinkles
that signaled your betrayal:
eye sockets of my perdition.

Oh dear, dear boy let's get
away on this train of air
from the civilization that bars us; let's welcome
the savage servitude in us devotedly,

at nighttime it's the silence that subdues
and kisses us and if you remain cold
then it's my fault, my mouth
doesn't kiss you or warm
your lips' embers.

But look, my boy: the night
has swaddled everything. The anguish
is perfect and no one else can shake it off
or dispossess it.

Imagine that I'm your mother and your little
siblings are so many small birds
with craws full of food and I'm their
brother and the Train Station the Pincio and the Coliseum

no longer matter to us.

Fosse l'ultimo amore il tuo
pure direi a me stesso: "Ama.

Soffrire è godimento, è pena:
tagliarsi le vene è saggio.
Non morire è un passo accorto
che puoi fare per coraggio
se morte è tutto, e nulla
è la vita."

Così ascolto le sirene dell'oltraggio
e tutto il pianto di cui ero capace
ormai fa parte di un viaggio
che non riguarda più la mia carcassa.

Ascetico e sensuale e senza tempo
vivo fra piazze e strade di Roma.

Ascolto voci sotterranee che dicono
che il mio giorno è finito. Ma vivo
resto e mi trascino in vita, cara
vita che persi tutta d'un botto

ferocemente entrando nella vita.

Del resto l'infanzia è lontana,
l'adolescenza sparita: la rappresentazione
è quasi finita. Signori, si chiude!

If yours were the last love
I would still say to myself: "Love.

Suffering is enjoyment, toil:
slitting one's wrists is wise.
Not dying is a rational move
that you make out of courage
if death is everything, and life
is nothing."

This is how I listen to the sirens of outrage
and all the tears of which I was capable
are by now part of a journey
that no longer matters to my carcass.

Ascetic and sensual and atemporal
I live among the piazzas and roads of Rome.

I listen to subterranean voices that tell me
my day is done. But I linger on
and I drag myself through life, dear
life where I lost everything all of a sudden

ferociously while being born.

Of what remains childhood is faraway,
adolescence gone: the performance
is almost done. Ladies and gentlemen, it's over!

La mattina, birre, "salade", un po' di caviale
o salmone. Non ero abituato a simile regime
alimentare, essendo di poveri trascorsi famigliari,
anche se dignitosi, senza elemosine stupide di
Dame di San Vicenzo frequentate da tu madre,
nobildonna ricchissima anche se con un falso
titolo nobiliare di contessa dei miei stivali.

Ero la tua vittima predestinata, la centesima
della tua calda estate di martire del pennello
falso-ideologico e del falso-erotismo
che va bene per una minoranza poco inquieta,
di quelle che frequentano i vespasiani e le latrine
di Borgo Pio, senza tanti complimenti per
il metraggio del sesso, tranne poi a scomparire
nei salotti borghesi delle finte aristocrazie
romane, come fecero un tempo i Trompeo,
o il famoso Palazzeschi sempre pronto a
ricevere in vestaglia i bei ragazzi.

In the mornings, beer, "salade," a bit of caviar
or salmon. I wasn't used to such eating
regimens, being of humble though dignified
familial means, without taking any trifling handouts from
the Sisters of Saint Vincent frequented by your filthy rich,
noblewoman of a mother with her fake
noble title of countess of my boots.

I was your predestined victim, the hundredth,
in the hot summer of your tight-fitting martyrdom
of false-ideology and false-eroticism
which works fine for those few barely fazed
by frequent trips to outdoor public toilets or the latrines
of Borgo Pio, without much worrying about
the tawdriness of sex, except afterward to disappear
into the bourgeois salons of the phony Roman
aristocracy, as long ago the Trompeos
or as the famous Palazzeschi did, always ready
in his dressing gown to entertain the pretty boys.

Libro d'amore (1982)

Lovebook

Nella mia notte il pessimo tuo mattino
sul lastrico mentre io vado a dormire
e tu non hai casa. Sei solo nel temporale.

Sì, nel lastrico, i marciapiedi a camminare,
sonno mai dormito per te. Invano io
nel letto e le sudate coperte

e tu mendichi a me piangendo la tua giornata
per accontentare la mia primordiale ferocità.

Che ora costringo il mio cattivo giorno all'aria
fino al castello delle tue ossa che un amante
inglese scrocchia.

Non c'è lutto per te, letto, usate
brande o mutande . . .

In my night the worst of your mornings
on the pavement while I go to sleep
and you have no home. You're alone in a storm.

Yes, on the pavement, sidewalks to walk,
sleep you never slept. Worthlessly I'm
in bed beneath sweaty bedcovers

and you beg to me whining about your day
to appease my primordial ferocity.

Now I'll confine this unkind day to the air
all the way to the castle of your bones that
an English lover stokes.

There's no mourning for you, or bed, used
bedframe or underwear . . .

Sulla mia vita scatenata non entri
più. Resti in agguato sulla porta

e bussi e pisci piano piano o forte
e quelle visibili righe che dallo scroscio
si formano allegre sotto la fessura
dell'entrata – effimere efemeridi
di un Tempo quando Eros
ci legava e io ti bevevo tutto.

Qualcuno inorridisce. Io tremo
esitando e fingo assente
la mia volontà e non apro.

Ho di te orrore che mi uccida
e pietà. L'omicidio è
suicidio – sfarzo di povero
matto dal volto ancora adolescente.

You no longer enter into my unraveled
Life. You wait in ambush at the door

and knock and piss slowly or loudly
while visible lines from the runoff
happily web beneath the entryway
crack—ephemeral chronicles
of a Time when Eros
bound us and I drank all of you.

Someone's horrified. I tremble
hesitating and pretend my desire's
gone and I don't open.

I'm terrified you might kill me
and I pity you. Murder is
suicide—spectacle of a poor madman
who still has an adolescent face.

Il passato delle felicità. La sigaretta
accesa dopo la congiunzione casuale
e orale. Tu nel letto a gambe semiaperte; –
incontro di materia, e il segno
della virilità ormai rimpiccolita,
tornata alla pigra quotidianità.

I critici malati d'immortalità:
regine dei giornali che sputano
sentenze mentre tu chiedi
una maglietta vecchia per andare
al mare dove non affoghi
bagnando le tue ali.

The passing of happiness. A cigarette
lit after a casual and oral
coupling. You in bed legs semi-splayed;—
a test of will, and the sign
of an already shrunken virility
returned to its idle dailiness.

The critics sickened by immortality:
queens of the tabloids that spit
judgments while you ask for
an old T-shirt to go
to the sea where you don't drown
while bathing your wings.

Di là ti masturbi senza lode
per la tua masturbazione. Poi
la luna mi sorride sprofondato
in un lupanare d'angoscia

Non è tuo quel bianco corpo
diventato brunito per il sole. Non è
mio. Basta, pietà. Che tutta
questa caducità mi riempia
fino a soffocare.

From the other room you masturbate without praise
for your masturbation. Afterward
the moon beams on me collapsed
in a brothel of anguish

That's not your white flesh
tanned by the sun. It's not
mine. Enough, pity. If only
this transience could permeate
me until I suffocate.

Dove riposi io guardo.
Maturo la vendetta e la scaldo
perché si plachi fino all'ultimo
bacio.

Come è diversa la ripetizione!
La fine dell'amore dopo l'amore,
quando il decrepito cuore sa

di poter battere in pace. Che
tranquillo l'aspetta
l'oscuro sonno animale!

Ora che tutto è vizzo e cerchiati
gli occhi non guardano che il vizio,

solo questo tempo di prede-caine
acqueta il canto delle Furie
furibonde di sapersi trascurate –

la sommossa certa orecchiabile
impunita del cazzo
che nelle braghette canta.

Where you sleep I watch over.
I ripen the vendetta and fuel it
till it's soothed by the last
kiss.

How strange this repetition!
The end of love after love,
when the decrepit heart knows

at last to beat in peace. How
peacefully that dark animal
sleep waits for him!

Now that everything's shriveled and squinting
eyes do nothing but seek out vice,

only this age of raising Cain
appeases the chanting of the Furies
rabid in their knowledge of being neglected—

the riot's certainly easy listening
unfazed by the cock
that in its codpiece sings.

Pallido, scarmigliato. I tuoi capelli
nelle mie mani aguzze come pugnali.

Il tuo sesso nelle mie mani, liscio,
pieno di seme da succhiare, in gola

piano scivolare. Le tue mani ora
tristemente fredde, inerti e come bava

il mio ricordo mentre cammino
fra un ponte e l'altro del Tevere.

Pale, disheveled. Your hair
in my hands sharp as daggers.

Your sex in my hands, smooth
full of seed to savor, in my throat

sliding slow. Your hands now
joylessly cold, inert and like drool

my memory while walking
from one bridge of the Tiber to another.

Le trombe squilleranno
l'incubo sordo
allora forse ti rivedrò
non più di carne
con un altro al lato
orgoglioso passerò senza saluti
nessuno più ci presenterà
il vituperio assordante
silenzioso impazzirà
i nostri detriti cervelli
dissepolti per l'ultima volta
in un'apocalisse irrisolta.

The trumpets will blare
the deaf specter
perhaps I'll see you again
no longer of flesh
with another at your side
contemptuously I'll pass without greeting
no one will introduce us anymore
the deafening silent
ridicule will rattle
our rubbled brains
disinterred for the last time
in an unresolved apocalypse.

Ti leccavo fra le sporche lenzuola.
Esploravo il tuo corpo, sommerso
rifugio al mio sesso rifiutato
era morbido il tuo corpo, tenero
rifugio inquieto, veloce
a penetrare nel mio corpo.

Ora non mi bastano i battuti
lungo il fiume, gracili pescatori,
possibili assassini, infingardi
e mutanti posizione, nel letto;
tu mi manchi in spirito
e dolcezza primitiva,
sesso piegato, fresco
ragazzo come cibo
da mangiarsi avidamente.

I licked you between dirty sheets.
I explored your body, submerged
refuge of my refused sex
your body was smooth, tender
a restless refuge, quick
to penetrate my body.

Now the tricks along the river
are not enough, ragged fishermen
possible assassins, indolent
and mutable position, in bed;
I miss you in spirit
and in primitive sweetness,
folded sex, fresh
boy like food
to eat hungrily.

io (1983)

i

POLVERE E CENERE

Ciò che in polvere è stremato
più di futuro non risorge
Chi è in Croce
alza gli occhi
e conta le costellazioni, almeno.

Beato chi è felice
a prevedere massacri
e strepiti e il nulla melodioso
inferno salutare.

Fragile me invece
che inginocchiarmi non so
sulla terra nuda e polverosa
e baciarla senza rancore
di doverci tornare.

ASHES AND DUST

What's commingled with dust
no longer rises in the future
Who's on the Cross
looks upward
and counts the constellations, at least.

Blessed the man who is glad
to foretell massacres
and clamor and greet the melodious
nothingness of hell.

I, on the other hand, am fragile
and do not know how to kneel
on this naked and dusty earth
nor kiss it without rancor
for a chance to return.

Non raggiungerò il Sublime perché sono vivo

Se sono vivo l'idea di morire che dietro
mi porto può sciagurare di continuo
come una Moira offesa e tremenda.
La verità è che non vivo, ma il calore
clandestino della Stufa che accendo
di nascosto del Signor Serafino
che mi sta su, sopra la testa
a controllare i miei sogni
mi riscalda ancora e scuote
il mio decrepito e impaurito
corpo terrorizzato di produrre
la vendetta suprema, lei, la morte,
la cammella idiota
che percorre deserti senz'acqua
e alla fine non vi scorre che il nulla
nel letto pietroso trovato

I will never arrive at the Sublime because I'm alive

If I am alive the idea of dying
which haunts me may continually devastate
like an offended and fearsome Goddess of Fate.
The truth is I do not live, but the clandestine
heat of the Stove I light
unknown to Mr. Seraphim
who lives above, upstairs
controlling my dreams
still rekindles and shakes
my decrepit and frightened
body terrified to produce
that supreme vendetta, you, death
idiotic camel
that roams the waterless deserts
where in the end only nothingness flows
in a stony uncovered bed

Penso che dovrei avere un figlio:
che mi guardi dal letto sfatto e sorrida
mentre ascolto una musica lontana
celestiale, di sogno . . . La porta
aperta sull'infinito, e un'infinita
preghiera . . . Calme parole
sussurrate nel vento aperto
della notte oscura. Io ti guardo,
figlio, dormiente sereno
in un tripudio colorato, mimetico
di rosse coperte, su un divano bianco
un cappelletto blu in testa
a coprire i capelli tagliati corti
come un collegiale o un militare.

Io solo, solissimo ti guardo,
figlio, non avendo doni per te
oggi che splende il tuo sedicesimo
compleanno. Non trovo
che sommesse virtù per rasserenarti
in un futuro che nessuna morte
intoccabile sfiorerà
con la sua adunca orrida mano.

I believe I should have a child:
who looks at me from the unmade bed and smiles
while I listen to a distant heavenly
music, dreamlike. . . . The door
opened onto the infinite, and an infinite
prayer . . . Calm words
whispered in the open wind
of a dark night. I look at you,
Son, sleeping serenely,
in colorful exultation, camouflaged
in red blankets, on a white couch
a little blue cap on your head
to cover your short haircut
like a prep schoolboy or a soldier.

Only me, all alone I look at you,
Son, not bearing any gifts for you
today on the occasion of your sixteenth
birthday. I can only manage
a few stifled virtues to soothe you
in a future where no death
no matter how untouchable escapes
the hooked horrid hand.

da *Gatti*

from *Cats*

Uscita da una tomba
al cimitero degli Inglesi
non so quanta durerai,
se un mese, se un anno:
resti solo tu àncora di salvezza
ad una vita incerta di domani

Exited from a tomb
at the English Cemetery
I don't know how long you'll last,
a month, a year:
you remain sole anchor of salvation
in a life uncertain of tomorrow

Rimorso a guardarti nella confusione;
sei solo una gatta, anzi sei una gatta,
una natura felice, un miracolo, un incanto:
quando agiti la coda o cerchi di afferrarla
sei più dispettosa di ogni ragazzo,
più dolce di ogni zucchero filato.
Ma il rimorso mi divora, sapessi,
pensando che dovrò lasciarti,
non sono fedele negli amori,
non so sacrificarmi.
Dimmi che fine farai
lasciami libero di decidere,
di perdermi in un altro destino.

I feel remorse looking at you confused;
you're only a cat, I mean, a cat,
a felicitous being, a miracle, an enchantment:
when you wag your tail and try to grab it
you're more spiteful than any boy,
sweeter than any cotton candy.
But remorse devours me, if you only knew,
thinking that I must leave you,
I'm not faithful in love,
I don't know how to sacrifice.
Tell me what will become of you
leave me free to decide,
to lose myself in another destiny.

Cessa di puntarmi come il cane
la sua preda: sono tuo ormai
e mai ti abbandonerò
fino alla fine dei miei o tuoi dì.
Infatti eccomi qua
tornato a posta per te, per darti
il prezioso cibo che ti tiene
in vita, te e il tuo piccolo figlio
adottivo preso di notte alla Stazione,
strappandolo da sicura morte

La famiglia si è accresciuta

io non sono più solo, a brandelli
lungo l'azzurro cielo.

Stop staring at me like a dog
does his prey: by now I'm yours
and I'll never abandon you
not till the end of my or your days.
In fact, here I am
returned just for you, to give you
the precious food that keeps you
alive, you and your little adoptive son
picked up at night at the Station
snatching him from certain death

The family has expanded

I am no longer alone, in tatters
beside a blue heaven.

Una giornata di maggio, piovosa
il cielo lassù senza speranza
incerto, timido di pioggia
da buttare purificando le Creature
Io passai, fantasma assorto
in un peccato paradisiaco
davanti a rovine antiche
e lì tre creaturine miagolanti
m'invitarono a soffrire con loro.
Erano dentro una busta di plastica:
umidi di guazza ma vivi, ed io
li raccolsi davanti a tutto
il concerto di gatti randagi
che aspettavano il cibo delle gattare
Io ero ormai un gatto: gli occhi
di sirena delle femmine–gatto
mi guardavano cantando mentre
accorrevo al trepido soccorso.
Io fuggivo con la busta, e le gatte
mi correvano dietro contente.
I ciechi pulcini si agitavano
in cerca delle poppe
che io non avevo, armandomi
di un sottile contagocce.
Fui certo di perdermi
in quell'universo gattesco . . .

May, a rainy day
the sky up there hopeless
uncertain, threatening rain
that will purge the Creatures
I passed, a phantom rapt
in paradisiacal sin
in front of ancient ruins
and there three little meowing creatures
invited me to suffer with them.
They were in a plastic bag:
clammy with dew but alive, and I
gathered them up before a whole
concert of stray cats
that waited for food from the cat ladies
I was by now a cat: eyes
of the siren cat-women
watched me singing while
I rushed anxious to help.
I ran off with the bag, and the cats
ran after me contented.
The blind kitties agitated about
looking for teats
that I didn't have, armed instead
with a thin eyedropper.
I was certain to lose myself
in that universe of cats . . .

La Gattità

È molto più gatto lui di lui . . .

Ma la gattità che cos'è? E dove
dovremo volteggiare per raggiungerla?
Io rispondo al querulo amico
che è dentro di me, o forse
nemico ai giorni e alle ore
della vita che passa senza speranza,
io appunto rispondo con sapienza
innocua e innocente; non lo so:
tanto mi basta sapere
che la gattità e un'entità
fissa e superba
di cui gli uomini sono
totalmente sprovvisti.

CATNESS

He's more of a cat than he is . . .

But what is catness? And how
should we turn about to achieve it.
I respond to my querulous friend
that it's within me, or perhaps
enemy of the days and hours
of life that passes without hope,
I respond precisely with innocuous
and innocent knowledge; I don't know:
at any rate, it's enough for me to know
that catness is a constant
and magnificent essence
of which men are
totally lacking.

Dura legge sapere che niente
potrà consolare il niente assoluto
che ci divora lontano dal mare
nelle sabbie ardenti, o nell'acque
sospirose di una fontana fresca
e salutare. Niente, dirò,
fra pietre immemoriali
che laggiù, nella mattutina
passeggiata, sedendomi
su uno scalino
di una scala lunga
come quella di Giacobbe
guardo.
Pietre, pietre, sconnesse
da secoli non più a venire,
ma venuti. Pietre
dure, energiche, maschili
che mi coprirete
non nel linciaggio finale
ma nel dolce sonno del niente
che nessuno vuole saper
persona vuole vedere.

Harsh law to know nothing
will console the absolute void
that devours us far from the sea
in the fiery sands, or in the water
gurgling from a cool, vitalizing
fountain. I'll say nothing
among immemorial stones
that I look at
down there during morning
walks, while I sit
on a step
of a tall ladder
like Jacob's.
Stones, stones, severed
by centuries no longer to come,
but past. Stones
strong, energetic, man's
that cover me
not as in a final lynching
but in the sweet sleep of the void
that no one wants to know,
no one wants to see.

Felice te passero (impudicizia mi spinge
a nominarti, un tempo in rima i poeti
solitari ti avrebbero in fretta salutato),
felice te che volteggi in cerca di cibo
nell'aria fredda di questo inverno
romano e non pensi beato alla tua
felicità felice di sogni e chimere
innocenti e serene. Io dai vetri
dentro una buia stanza piango
i miei anni spariti – l'affanno,
l'affanno al cuore tormentato
mi dà male, mi uccide tanto
da morire di dolore, ma non muoio
mai, lo grido ai miei nemici
di sempre che urlano la mia diversità
nei salotti della Capitale ...

Happy sparrow (shamelessness drives me
to call your name, once in rhyme solitary
poets would have hurriedly greeted you),
happy being that flits about in search of food
in the cold air of this Roman
winter and doesn't worry, lucky you, thanks
to your overjoyed bliss of dreams
and serene innocent chimeras. From the windows
of a dark room I mourn
my lost years—the angst,
the wheezing of a tormented heart
causes me grief, slays me to the brink
of death from pain, but I don't die
ever, I shout this to my sworn
enemies who bemoan my queerness
in the parlors of the Capital . . .

LA FINE DEL MONDO

La fine, la fine è prossima . . .

La fine del Mondo; la natura
non e più matrigna, ma calpestata
distrutta denuncia al Creatore
l'uomo miserabile e indegno
che calpestandola, offendendola
la uccide. Moriremo tutti
presi come topi in una trappola:
forse è la morte mia
che mi spaventa e la unisco
a quella del Mondo, forse
e la mia morte e fuggo
per non nominarla, e
non mi lascio andare
alla memoria dei sogni
immateriali, nutrendo il corpo
dei giorni passati.
Non bisogna vivere di rimpianti:
la morte dei poeti è sicura
scrivere non basta più
ma e l'unica cosa che avanza
oltre la paura già cominciata
già accresciuta nel suo farsi
condanna e piacere della condanna.

The End of the World

The end, the end is near . . .

The end of the World: nature
is no longer rotting, but trampled
destroyed, it denounces the Creator
the miserable and unworthy man
who, trampling and offending her,
kills her. We'll all die
snared like rats in a trap:
perhaps it's my death
that frightens me and I link
it to the death of the World, perhaps
it's my death and I run away
so as not to call it by name, and
I don't allow myself to consider
the memory of immaterial
dreams, nourishing my body
with bygone days.
It's not necessary to live with regret:
the death of poets is certain
writing is no longer enough
but it's all that endures
beyond the already begun fear
intensified by its own becoming
condemnation and the pleasure of condemning.

Quando si abbandona la strada
certa per l'incerta anche gli amici
ti abbandonano o i lettori
che è peggio. Quando si parla
solo a se stessi, con ossessa
ripetizione della voglia
di farsi male alle radici
allora sì che resta solo
chi vuole bere la cicuta
fino in fondo . . .

When you abandon the certain
road for the uncertain even friends
abandon you or your readers do
which is worse. When you speak
only to yourself, with obsessive
repetition about the need
to hurt yourself down to your core
then yes all that's left
is he who wants to drink hemlock
to the last drop . . .

Non c'è niente di meglio che barare:
stare in cucina cucinando un minestrone.
Si svuoterà il frigo zeppo di cicoria,
pomodori passati, carote e zucchine:
si aspetterà l'ospite passando la cera
dando da mangiare al gatto caccoloso
raccolto a Campo dei Fiori, anzi offerto
da un ragazzo riapparso nel tempo
un fulgore del ricordo mai assaporato
veramente, non vivendo più in elemosina
ma modestamente, disprezzando da solo
i ricchi, fuggendo catene di denunce
per corruzione. Sì, non resta
che starsene in casa aspettando il freddo,
annunciando al mondo la propria rinuncia,
incontrando talvolta qualche poetessa
nemica, e andando a Porta Portese
alla ricerca di una buona coperta
di lana. Il gatto farà le fusa
d'inverno, con circospezione:
ancora è malato, il naso bruciato
dall'acqua ossigenata presa
per acido borico. Il trionfo vero
è quello della quotidianità.

There's nothing better to barter:
to be in the kitchen cooking minestrone.
You'll empty the fridge packed with chicory,
pureed tomatoes, carrots, and zucchini:
and wait for the guest by waxing the floors
and feeding the matted cat
picked up at Campo dei Fiori, gifted rather
by a boy who reappeared at the time
in a splendor of memory never actually
relished, as he was no longer living on charity
but getting by, singlehandedly scorning
the rich as they escaped scores of corruption
charges. Yes, all that remains
is to stay inside the house waiting for the cold,
announcing to the world its own renunciation,
occasionally meeting some enemy poetess,
and going to the Porta Portese
flea market in search of a good
wool blanket. In winter, the cat
will purr, suspiciously:
it's still sick, its nose burnt
from the hydrogen peroxide
I confused with boric acid. The real
triumph is that of the quotidian.

Serpenta (1987)

Snakewoman

Lingua, tu non rispondi, né apri
alle mie giornate la verità; ora mi spengo
in questo assorto tramonto di speranze
cercando la vita smarrita, il sole funesto
e sporco di un pomeriggio invernale:
la luce negli occhi di un Dio che è sparito.

Così Lingua, ti evoco, per immortalarti
ma è indubbio il tuo cascare in folle
verso memorie e ricordi particolari,
verso l'invasamento parziale di un'anima
che non sa esser anima di tutto il mondo:
anima, anima spenta che non cresce
delirando.

Tongue, you do not respond, nor unleash
the truth to my days; now I extinguish
myself in this rapt hopeful sunset
looking for the lost way, the woeful
and murky sun of a winter afternoon:
the light in the eyes of a God who's disappeared.

Therefore Tongue, I evoke you, to immortalize you
but your plummet into folly is undeniable
toward memories and specific remembrances,
toward the partial invasion of a soul
that does not know how to be the world's soul:
soul, dissipated soul that does not thrive
in its delirium.

Ma il quotidiano insiste. Ed io volo
verso il tarlo segreto della notte
per non saperne di più. Insiste così
il quotidiano, e stinge addosso la sua pece
o pace perduta, incontrando i mostri
attigui dell'eros metropolitano
che ormai costano troppo sul mercato
degli schiavi. Insiste dunque il quotidiano:
la poesia è merce o merda, voli di gabbiani
in tempesta mentre si pensa a sorella Morte,
o la Musa vagante in clinica, in crisi
di astinenza, l'astinente essendo io
gioioso immondo testimone di un giorno
di pioggia: calamitoso e sventurato giorno
solfeggiando in mortale voragine il buio
di domani o ieri o il tempo che scorre
verso eternità imprendibili.

But the quotidian insists. And I fly
toward the secret wormhole of night
in order not to know it anymore. It insists
the quotidian, and bleeds its pitch on you
or its displaced peace, while meeting monsters
next to the metropolitan Eros
that by now costs too much on the market
of slaves. Thus the quotidian insists:
poetry is commodity or crap, flights of seagulls
in a storm while thinking about sister Death,
or the stray Muse in the clinic, in a crisis
of abstinence, the abstinent being me
joyful foul witness of a rainy day:
disastrous and unfortunate day
bellowing from a fatal chasm the darkness
of tomorrow or yesterday or of time rushing
toward unattainable eternities.

Se è giovanetto il corpo maschile
risplende di luce incerta, ma chiara
guardate la mano con le linee appena
tracciate, e lungi il bisogno
di saperne di più. Informa il sesso
tutto il sotto muliebre ed efebico
in attesa di farsi uomo, maschio
altezza d'usignolo

If the male body is boyish
it gleams with tentative, but clear light
look at the hand with its lines barely
traceable, and far from the need
to know more. He'll coax his sex
below all womanly and ephebic
waiting to become man, male
at the height of a nightingale

Né maschile né femminile, il suo sguardo.
Di fuori l'aria serena invade
la realtà. Io non vedo, cieco
da sempre; mi sfiguro a pensare
i lieti conforti di una età diversa,
priva del vizio della morte.

Neither male nor female, that gaze.
From outside the serene air invades
reality. I don't see, blind
from the beginning; I deface myself to think
about the happy comforts of a different age,
devoid of death's vice.

Ragazzo laggiù, tesoro nascosto
col tuo gambo manichino
appoggiato al cuore, manovrato
per prima da te, o scempio delle borghesie
inani e gagliarde che vogliono il mio sangue!
Sì, manipolato per prima da te, ma calme
quelle notti con te che ritornavi
tardi . . . Era gioventù, passione
ladra di eventi strani, straordinari;
chitarre e vino, pane e insalata
e vittoria sul tuo corpo
martoriato dal Desiderio . . .

Vivrò nel tuo compianto
aspettando celesti punizioni
per la mia labilità, ma non sono più
poeta d'amore, né un sollievo
all'oggi mi dà rievocare il Passato.
Chiudo gli occhi, e penso potessi
ritornare com'ero! Come non sarò più.

Hey boy down there, hidden treasure
with your mannequin's limb
bent against your heart, manhandled
first by you, o mangle of the inane
and impudent middle classes that want my blood!
Yes, manipulated by you first, but calmly
those nights you returned
late . . . Youthful, thieving passion
of strange, extraordinary events;
guitar and wine, bread and salad,
and victory over your body
martyred by Desire . . .

I'll live within your regrets
awaiting celestial punishment
for my instability, but I'm no longer
a poet of love, nor does today's
solace conjure the Past.
I close my eyes, and think if only I could
return to what I was. As I will never be again.

AD HART CRANE

Terribile Eros, o angoscia
angoscia, gioia del sesso
poco prima che lo tocchi l'eccesso!

Mutante, ascoltami; mutante perdimi
quando il ragazzo mattutino
rischiara il suo volto magro
di sfortuna, viene, sviene, rinviene
nel letto caldo di mattino
a piangere il suo ardore
che corre lento, senza sensualità
puro niente innamorato da sé
e basta!

Così gridasti Hart, o caro Hart
poeta americano morto suicida
così gridasti al vento notturno
dal gran ponte precipitando
nell'abisso funereo della notte.

To Hart Crane

Terrible Eros, oh anguish
anguish, joy of sex
just before you touch his excess!

Changeable one, listen to me, changeable one
destroy me as the boy's thin face daily
brightens with misfortune,
he comes, he faints, he revives
in the warm morning bed
to cry his ardor
that flows slowly, without sensuality
or purity in love with himself alone
and nothing else!

That's how you cried out Hart, dear Hart
American poet dead by suicide
that's how you cried to the nocturnal wind
from the great precipitous bridge
into the funereal abyss of night.

A Pier Vittorio Tondelli

Il Tevere si perde nella notte.
Il vento sforza la tua bocca
di miele; assaporo dal vivo
le rose languide della tua primavera.

Il passo rapido di un poliziotto
forse giovane e indulgente, forse
vecchio che fruga le scalette
confonde i ricordi e il cielo
diventa più nero –

Pazzo, pazzo d'amore, d'amare
porte ignaro mercante rabbioso
dove entro senza cercare al buio
di me silenzioso amante, grido
alla meta dei giorni, a metà
della vita arrivato e sazio,
oscuro ancora a me stesso
l'inquieto, intriso filo del sesso –
sento d'abbandonare i casi personali,
abiurare, rinnegare le celesti sfere
dell'ozio notturno o del narciso infetto.
Calpesterò la Storia
per vergogna o diletto.

For Pier Vittorio Tondelli

At night we lose sight of the Tiber.
The wind forces open your honeyed
mouth; I taste firsthand
the languid roses of your springtime.

The quick pace of a police officer
perhaps young and willing, or maybe
elderly who gropes for the stairs
confounds the memories and the sky
goes dark—

Crazed, crazed for love, to love
thresholds oblivious and rabid for trade
where I enter without looking for the gloom
within, muted lover, I shout
to get through the days, arrived
midway through life and sated,
but still unknown to myself
restless, high-wired for sex—
inclined to abandon personal grievance,
to abjure, repudiate the celestial spheres
of nightly idleness or of infected Narcissus.
I'll trample History
out of dishonor or delight.

Sottoponte
Ad Aldo Busi

Notturno orinatoio autunnale
nella sera fredda dai tersi colori
nella notte che cala senza fretta,
dove un ragazzo passa –
gli occhi umidi, cerchiati e irraggiungibili
dell'innocenza più pura di pietà –
la carità, l'obolo dell'eros concedi
a quanti infreddoliti questuanti, furtivi
passanti del marciapiede più indulgente
ai passi strascicati, maniaci, derelitti
ai passi veloci per scendere le scale
che portano al ponte delle abominazioni:
superbia di chiedere alla strage paterna
degli idoli, alla notturna, dolcissima
religio.

Mano materna e umile sottoponte,
accompagna il canto dei condannati
nell'umidità secca e scandita
nel batticuore dai rumori più intollerabili,
deciso a palpitazioni più veloci
per la cattiva polizia che s'aggira!
Dove allora si dirige la rivalità ilare
dei perduti,
delle pazze smaniose di carneficina
che la tranquillità polverosa di pescatori
seduti sul bordo del fiume
a contemplare l'acqua lucida di stelle
allontana da qualche soave metro, –
tracotanti di malafede per qualche
creatura teneramente affaticata
dal suo segreto seme disperatamente
disputato?

BELOW BRIDGE
For Aldo Busi

Nightly autumnal urinal
in the cold night of crisp colors
in the night that descends listlessly
where a boy passes by—
his damp eyes, dark-circled and inaccessible
with an innocence purer than pity—
you offer charity, the erotic bribe
to how many shivering vagrants, furtive
passersby on the sidewalk more forgiving
to shuffling, maniacal, derelict footsteps
to the quick paces descending the stairs
that lead to the bridge of abominations:
haughtily to ask for the paternal carnage
of idols, of the sweetest nightly
reverence.

A motherly and humble hand below bridge,
accompanies the canto of the condemned
in the damp and rhythmic shoals
in the racing heart of the most intolerable clatter,
set on even faster palpitations
because of the bullying police roaming about!
Where does this hysterical rivalry
of the damned lead,
from mad women anxious for slaughter
to the mucky tranquility of fishermen
sitting on the edge of the river
to contemplate the water lucid with stars
at some slight distance away,—
contemptuous with bad faith for some
poor creature tenderly fatigued
by his desperately contested
secret seed?

Fuggono tutti i giorni miei
o oscura luce dagli occhi incantatori.
Fuggono, si perdono, corrono
dietro le immagini di una volta:
i baci, gli abbracci, i turbamenti
insinceri del ragazzo migliore
fuggono atterriti verso la fine
che è prossima. Solo tu, Serpenta,
gioisci e mi riscuoti come larva
che al sole si sveglia e vola via

All my days escape
o dark light of incantatory eyes.
They escape, are lost, chase
behind images of a past time:
the kisses, the embraces, the insincere
turmoil of the best boyfriend
escapes terrified toward the end
which is imminent. Only you, Snakewoman,
rejoice and rouse me like larva
that in the sun spawns and flies away

Quando sarai chiamata in Paradiso (perché
ci andrai a raggiungere gli amati gatti)

un'eco immensa ti avvertirà di essere arrivata:
un'eco sprigionata dall'Eterno Felice
per ringraziarti umilmente di avere con pietà
scritto, scriba zingaresca intossicata da Talmud
e Scienze del Profondo, un libro, il Libro, divino
per innocenti lettori, mille per mille, ed io
con questi; ti arriverà anche una vocina,
la mia, di topo purgatoriale e lontano
in attesa del perdono nuziale; io che mischiai
la mia, di voce, al coro degli applausi
e poi si confuse davanti allo strepito
dei negatori malati d'invidiosa barbarie:
frettolosi lettori di un messaggio invivibile
dentro i cieli e le brume della mortifera terra.

Dunque sta' tranquilla, nella tua solitaria stanza;
quello che dovevi fare hai compiuto in perfetta armonia:

la tua vita non è passata invano fra i terrestri.

When you are called to Paradise (because
you'll go there to meet up with your beloved cats)

a tremendous echo will signal your arrival:
an echo emanating from Eternal Bliss
to thank you humbly for having written with compassion,
gypsy-esque scribe intoxicated by the Talmud
and Sciences of the Profound, one book, the Book, divine
for innocent readers, by the thousands, and I
among them; a tiny voice will also reach you,
mine, of a purgatorial and faraway mouse
waiting for eternal forgiveness; I who mixed
my voice, with the chorus of applause
and then it was lost in front of the clamor
of the naysayers sick with envious barbarism:
heedless readers of an untenable message
in the hazy heavens of a lethal earth.

Rest assured, now, in your solitary room;
what you meant to do you did in perfect harmony:

your life did not pass in vain among the living.

Libro di poesia (1990)

Poetry Book

LACRIMA AMORIS

Come si fa a resistere alle lacrime?

Sono radioattive ormai come il cuore
dopo Chernobyl: oggi non piange più nessuno:
neppure i morti sono pianti, anche la Signora

Eccelsa di nome Morte non piange. Ma io
alle lacrime non so rinunciare, alle lacrime
piante per finta o per davvero condite
di perfidi pulviscoli non so rinunciare.
Le calde lacrime che su gote amate
scendono piano o silenziose
come una mano le scalda un'altra
le butta via. Lacrime leccate, invano
succhiate che resistono alla vita,
si spargono in lacrime purulente
come lacrime venute a pioggia
da un mondo lontano e infetto.

Si piange, e chi piange nell'attesa
non può vincere il pianto. L'Intrattabile
è morto: radiazioni illacrimate
lo spensero nel diluvio della pioggia:

io non piango un pianto contaminato,
né posso raccogliere il tuo pianto
radioattivo che scende, sì, su gote amate
ormai avvelenate, baciate su dita
aride e consunte, contate avido
di essere vicino alla contaminazione
finale, o Chernobyl di morte
più mortale di un cuore desolato
e assente.

Lacrima Amoris

How can we resist tears?

They're radioactive by now like the heart
after Chernobyl: today no one cries anymore
not even the dead are mourned, even the Exalted

Lady named Death doesn't cry. But I
do not know how to renounce tears, I don't know
how to renounce tears cried falsely or actually
seasoned by perfidious dust.
Fiery tears that fall slow and silent
on beloved cheeks
warmed by one hand while another
wipes them away. Tears licked, in vain
sucked in that defy life,
they spread as purulent tears
like tears come as rain
from a faraway and infected world.

We cry, and they who cry in anticipation
cannot conquer the grief. The Intractable
is dead: he perished in unmourned radiation
in the flood of rain:

I don't cry a contaminated cry
nor can I hoard your radioactive
tears that fall, yes, down beloved cheeks
already poisoned, kissed on gaunt and
wasted fingers, avid effects
of being close to the final
contamination, o Chernobyl of death
more mortal than a desolate
and missing heart.

La mia casa, l'entrata

Ho scritto svariate poesie sulla mia casa.
Ma nessuna sulla sua porta d'entrata –
l'ho ridipinta di bianco, accecando
un senso irreale e sospeso. Qualcuno
potrà capire oscuri sentimenti, di morte
invocata, affrettata; a me piace così,
bianca e puttana se dà il viatico
solenne ad una vita sbagliata:
la mia perdizione, il poco cercasi –
la solitudine del creato rimbomba
sulla soglia maledetta, l'assassino
lo sento sempre in agguato; i gatti
lontani, abbandonati al giustiziere
delle notti inutili. Così non cerco
più di rimestare nel torbido, mi dico
solo, sono a casa, nella parte più
minacciata, nella parte più stregata
dove tutti mi possono trovare. Sia,
quando arrivo, quando esco trafelato,
perduta ogni dimora, ogni entrata!
Sia smarrita la volontà di vivere
gli storti sogni o la calamità;
chiunque entri, oppure nessuno;
la porta sia chiusa per sempre
come dopo la morte terrestre,
dei sensi; sulla soglia inviolata
resti solo la paura ricercata
come una rosa profumata. Resti, sì
l'angoscia, la furia, la bestialità
di un attimo già vissuto
guardando un corridoio regale,
brutale – regalo agli occhi

My House, the Entrance Way

I have written various poems about my house.
But none about its front door—
I repainted it white, a blinding
sense of unreality and suspension. Someone
may comprehend its obscure notions, of death
invoked, hurriedly; I like it like that,
white and whorish if it offers a solemn
viaticum for a wronged life:
my perdition, cared about little—
the solitude of this handiwork resounds
on the accursed doorstep, the assassin
I sense always in ambush; the cats
faraway, forsaken to the vigilante
of futile nights. In this way I no longer
try to stir up the tumult, I tell myself
alone, I'm home, in the part most
threatened, the part most haunted
where everyone can find me. Whether
I arrive, or leave out of breath,
every home, every entrance is lost!
May the will to endure twisted
dreams or calamity disappear;
whoever enters, or if no one does;
may the door be closed forever
as after the earthly death,
of the senses; on the unsullied threshold
may only the sought-after fear remain
like a perfumed rose. Yes, may
the anguish, fury, and barbarity
of a moment already gone also endure
while staring at a regal, brutal
corridor—a feast for the eyes

Un trasloco

Ho sognato un trasloco (quale? dirà il lettore,
il vizio peggiore è mettersi dalla sua parte,
ignorando le ragioni del cuore) come fosse
l'ultimo giorno di una vita illusa e feroce;
l'ultimo giorno in cui ancora abbiamo la forza
smisurata e imprendibile di dire a chi passa:
"Vieni su, conosciamoci!" Tenera, tenera
infanzia malata che ritorna! E ho troppa
paura del futuro per vivere solo nel passato:
per dimenticare i momenti eterni di una casa
ove si compie nel sacro mistero della poesia
l'incarnazione mia definitiva, estremo viaggio
nella vita di poi; mentre di là
oltre il ponte Sisto e il cielo di rugiada
splende una casa ignota a me, senza un contratto,
uno straccio di contratto eslege; passaporto
per una rinascita imminente ma rifiutata.
Meglio sarebbe stato restare così; addormentarsi
piano nella veglia funebre di un forno abitudinario
sotto che intossicava i miei polmoni gracili,
permettendomi tenaci fughe verso l'amato Sud:
Calabrie, Sicilie, Lucanie, Pantellerie.
L'orrore, nella vita è decidere, cambiare,
abituarsi al meglio che è il peggio per chi
non è più giovane, viaggiatore d'ombre al passo
di marcia sbagliato.

A Relocation

I dreamt of a move (which one? the reader will ask,
the worst habit is to put oneself in his place,
ignoring the reasons of the heart) as if it were
the last day of a deluded and ferocious life;
the last day we still have the limitless
and irresistible strength to say to who passes:
"Come up, let's meet!" Tender, tender
sickly infancy that returns! And I have too much
fear of the future to live only in the past:
to forget the eternal moments in a house
where in the sacred mystery of poetry I complete
my definitive incarnation, the extreme journey
to the life after; while from there
beyond the Sixtus Bridge and the sultry sky
a house unknown to me gleams, without a lease,
a tatter of a lawless contract; a passport
for an imminent but refused rebirth.
Better to have remained like this; to fall asleep
slowly in the funerary wake of a habitual furnace
below which my frail lungs were poisoned,
requiring regular getaways toward the beloved South:
the Calabrias, Sicilys, Lucanias, Pantellerias.
The horror of life is to decide, to change,
to get used to the best which is the worst for those
no longer young, traveler of shadows moving
in the wrong gear.

AIDS

Il mio AIDS, alla Francese SIDA,
come dire Madame Sida, buongiorno!,
non esiste –
anche se insiste sulla terra:
vola in alto il virus che uccide
i vecchi peccatori di un attimo

Non ne sarò premiato
come unica tomba la tomba
poi il silenzio che verrà:
il che è la stessa cosa più alta
e sottile nel creato immondo
e votato a distruzione
per atomico oltraggio

ultima sirena della fine

Dunque fuggiamo, o AIDS,
disamori e cecità manifeste
il languore dei secoli spenti
in un abbraccio salutare; chiudiamo
nel cuore un ragazzo felice
e sbarazzino, volante, esibizionista
senza sparare niente se t'insinui
nelle crepe della carne;
fuggire non vale, se scomparire
non puoi riscaldarmi con fiducia
bevimi, leccami pure

AIDS

My AIDS, in French SIDA,
as if to say good morning!, Madame Sida,
doesn't exist—
even if it persists on earth:
it hovers above this virus that kills
old sinners of an instant

I won't be awarded
its unique tomb the tomb
where afterward silence attains:
which is equivalent but loftier
and subtler in foul creation
and dedicated to destruction
by atomic disaster

last siren of the end

Let us escape then, o AIDS,
disaffection and blindness manifest
the languor of spent centuries
in a healthy embrace; let's shut
a happy and playful boy, a carefree
and exhibitionistic one in our hearts
without shooting up anything if you infiltrate
the cracks of the flesh;
escape is futile, if you can't
disappear warm me confidently
drink me, lick me even

I GIOVANI PADRI

Io, eroe notturno, notturnamente ero
solare se m'imbattevo in qualche giovane padre!

Sono state le mie lacrime, stanotte,
a ricordarmi che ho amato un giovane
padre – quasi come fosse un ragazzino
nervoso e ilare perché la paternità
lo rendeva libero e io ero sua madre.

Il mio destino, la mia molteplicità
sa che non sarò mai padre. È io

mi sussurro questo nome e la notte
tocco nel mio letto vuoto il sesso
di uno che lo è stato e forse lo sarà.

Dura vita, infinita infinità di morte:
calmo appuntamento. Appressamento
rotto dal desiderio-compassione
d'un giovane padre: i corti capelli,

le mani virili, il sorriso
senza dissociazioni col suo sesso.
La speranza a renderlo più forte
di qualsiasi figlio. La normalità.

I giovani padri! I battiti del loro cuore
sono l'amorosità delle rivoluzioni!

I loro bambini sono
le speranze dell'umanità. Il loro seme
per l'uomo oscurato dal male
è la libertà. I ragazzi devono
sforzarsi di diventare come loro,

THE YOUNG FATHERS

I, nocturnal hero, nightly
beamed if I came across some young father!

They were my tears, tonight,
that reminded me I loved a young
father—almost as if he were a young boy
nervous and exhilarated because fatherhood
rendered him free and I was his mother.

My destiny, my diversity
tells me I'll never be a father. And I

murmur his name to myself and at night
in my empty bed I touch the sex
of someone who has been a father or will be.

Harsh life, infinite infinity of death:
a calm appointment. Whose approach
is broken by the desire-compassion
for a young father: the short hair,

the manly hands, the smile
without disassociating from his sex.
The hope to render him stronger
than any son. This normalcy.

Young fathers! The beating of their hearts
is the magnanimity of revolutions!

Their children are
the hope of humanity. Their seed
for the man obscured by evil
is freedom. Boys need
to force themselves to become like them,

contenere la futura virilità.
Per questo non sono disponibili. Sono malati.

Ma i giovani, i giovani padri
hanno mutato la città, ospedale-città
in una rugiada se solo passano
coi lor figli a tracollo e le madri spente
a lato a vivere di questa maternità.

I giovani padri io attraverso e brucio
col fuoco della mente, in un pianeta diverso
da questo pieno d'Orfei, dove conta la forza
della procreazione e la sterilità di primavera
è un campo di concentramento per traditori.

to contain a future virility.
Yet, they're not willing. They're sickly.

But the young, the young fathers
have turned the city, the hospital-city
into mist merely by passing
with their sons on their backs and spent
mothers by their side living this maternity.

I go through and burn young fathers
with the fire of my mind, in a planet queerer
than this one full of Orpheuses, where the force
of procreation counts and the sterility of spring
is a concentration camp for traitors.

Pratiche attività

Perché se il poeta è ridotto a svolgere
pratiche attività, a tenersi in vita
telefonando, brigando, lavorando
ahimè contro Dio, o il dio
più minuscolo della poesia, a chi
farne colpa? Oppure andando
d'inverno, al freddo tiepido
di gennaio inoltrato verso Campo
e incontrando un giovane passato
nel vero campo del crimine
che ti desidera lungo il fiume
molle, fra la fanga, al vento
entrando, squartando, uscendo
in mirabilia di seme, di chi
è la colpa?
Ma passano i giorni, la vita
senza lamentarsi, confortando
l'idea che la vita davanti ancor c'è,
è lunga, anche se domani potremmo
morire, sfiatando

PRACTICAL ACTIVITIES

If the poet is reduced to carrying out
practical activities, to get by
using the phone, hustling, working
even against God, or the more
lowercase one of poetry, who
should we blame? Or if by going
in winter, into the tepid cold
in the heart of January toward Campo dei Fiori
you meet a young man who's passed by
crime's true domain
and craves you along the slack
river, in the muck, wind
encroaching, ripping you apart, leaving
awestruck by cum, who is
to blame?
But the days pass, a lifetime
without complaint, comforted by
the idea that there's still life ahead,
and it's long, even if tomorrow we could
die, just breathing

COLOSSEO

Colosseo che mi hai cresciuto agli Amori
rientro in te come nel ventre di una Madre;
lascio indietro il patetico piccolo mondo
che m'offende; si allenta il rumore
del traffico, delle macchine che sobillano
la coscienza insicura di sé a desiderarle.

Tutto velocemente cambia, il destino si perde
dentro gli umidi corridoi, ritorna
all'unica sorte possibile: la carne
fa strazio di sé per punirsi di crescere,
o di essere cresciuta al Desiderio e al Potere.

Eppure sono ancora povero come un monaco
che abbia fatto un patto diabolico con la Povertà:
ma già nel non ritornare più ragazzo, nel
non essere, come allora, piagato e visitato
dai sogni irrisolti del sesso ancora pieno
di mistero – aperto alla vita proprio
perché più chiuso, più umiliato e stanco,
mi sono perduto, non sono più il tentato,
una cavia potenziale di tutto l'inautentico
e il disumano, ma colui che possiede, nella
mente, la verità del proprio misero fato
depositato nel falso mistero d'un sesso troppo
svelato se qui facilmente lo incontro, in questo
luogo millenario, quasi eterno, e lo compro . . .
Nel mentre forse i miei più puri compagni,
della loro richiesta d'intelligenza
fanno la sofferenza più atroce della loro vita,
si sdanno nei riti brutali dei cortei
che protestano la democrazia proletaria.
La democrazia borghese permette la mia esistenza

COLISEUM

Coliseum that's helped me grow accustomed to Lovers
I reenter you as into the womb of a Mother;
I leave behind the pathetic bourgeois world
that offends me; the traffic noise eases,
from cars that stir up the uncertain
consciousness of self toward its own desire.

Everything quickly changes, destiny is lost
within your humid corridors, it returns
to its only possible lot: the flesh that
tortures itself to punish itself from growing,
or from being raised by Desire and by Power.

And yet I'm still as poor as a monk
who's likely made a diabolical pact with Poverty:
but already by not returning as a boy, by
not being, as I was then, plagued and visited
by irresolute dreams of sex still full
of mystery—open to life exactly because
I'm more shut down, more humiliated and tired,
I've lost myself, I'm no longer the tempted one,
a potential guinea pig of all the inauthentic
and the inhuman, but instead he who possesses, within
the mind, the truth of his own miserable fate
consigned to the false mystery of a sex too
revealed if here I encounter it readily, in this
millennial, almost eternal place, and I buy it . . .
In the meantime, perhaps my purest friends,
in their quest for intelligence
create the most atrocious suffering of their lives,
by coming undone in brutal rites of procession
which protest proletarian democracy.
Bourgeois democracy allows for my existence

e di questa diversità neutralizzata fa l'alibi
della sua sopravvivenza; e così accetto
perché costretto questo sistema che pur mi ripugna
come oggetto, reale, delle mie repulsioni senza
speranza, come l'adempimento del mio diseredato
destino di cavia non più cavia, ma votato
ad un impoetico messaggio, impopolare e superbo,
che della borghesia fa la categoria universale
perché necessaria alla sua sopravvivenza.
Lì, in un mondo diverso, forse più giusto,
meno alienato di questo, io non avrei diritto
neppure alla vita, non tanto perché diverso
ma perché soffocato da questa diversità a
toccare con mano la reale sanità degli uomini
nutriti di giustizia e libertà. Qui,
nel decrepito, fatiscente mondo tutte le diversità
proprio perché tali, politiche, razziali, sessuali,
sono epifenomeni di una stessa angoscia
che fa esister: quella del neo-capitalismo,
della borghesia che ha paura dei mostri
che essa produce. Ma lì
in un mondo di eguali, dove i mostri
tutti dalla ragione saranno esorcizzati,
io stesso come prolungamento abietto
d'un mondo maledetto dovrò da solo,
prima che qualcuno me lo ordini, ammazzarmi.
Qui sono un ricattatore, lì sarei un ricattato:
nessun'altra sorte mi è concessa.
Fra le tue pietre, Colosseo, mi sento sicuro
come il Delfino nella sontuosa reggia
del re suo padre. Tutto mi è familiare:
il buco più otturato ha visto i miei occhi
indagatori cercare il segno della dolce
perversione, del sesso maleducato,
che si nutre, si attossica, la notte,
quando le luci sono spente, e iniziano

and of this nullified diversity it creates alibis
of its own survival; and as such because I'm forced to,
I accept this system that still disgusts me
as a manifestation, of my own repulsions without
hope, as with the fulfillment of my disinherited
destiny of guinea pig no longer a guinea pig, but devoted
to an unpoetic, unpopular, and haughty slogan
that for the bourgeoisie becomes a universal
category necessary to its survival.
There, in a different world, perhaps more righteous
less alienated than this one, I wouldn't have the right
even to life, not so much because I'm different
but because I'm suffocated by this queer need to
touch by hand the real health of men
nourished on justice and liberty. Here,
in the decrepit, decaying world all diversities
exactly because they are similar, political, racial, sexual,
are epiphenomena of one singular anguish
that allows for existence: that of neo-capitalism,
of the bourgeoisie that fears the monsters
it itself produces. But there
in a world of equals, where the monsters
all will be exorcised by reason,
I myself as the vile extension
of a damned world should on my own,
before someone orders me, kill myself.
Here I am a blackmailer, there I'm blackmailed:
no other lot is granted to me.
Among your rocks, Coliseum, I feel secure
like the Dauphin in the sumptuous royal palace
of the king, his father. Everything is familiar to me:
the hole most plugged up has seen my probing
eyes search for a sign of sweet
perversion, of raunchy sex,
that nurtures itself, that poisons, at night,
when the lights are out, and they begin

i riti teneri e imbecilli, di incontinenze
e di facili erezioni, di seme acido
da tranghiottirsi in fretta e senza fretta,
a seconda che qualche concorrente s'aggiri,
o la polizia travestita da ossessa, vecchia
zia da Ospizio per vecchi in cerca di qualcuno
biondo o bruno, brutale e aitante,
scappato dall'Inferno del Riformatorio
e cascato in quest'altro Inferno, meno coatto
certo, ma più desolato, dove la solitudine
più spaventosamente sola, dell'anima
e del corpo, ti possiede intero, non muta
mai alla speranza di un incontro fortunato.

Qui, tutto, Colosseo, è in funzione dell'erezione
e guai a quello che per la prima volta s'inoltra
a provocare coi baci sulla bocca tante, esauste
eiaculazioni, insieme alla sua, prima e ultima.
Ma perché io cerco qui quello che mai troverò?
Per quale autolesionistico, inesorabile mistero?
Qui, in te, pur tornando ragazzo, non torno più
ragazzo, come una volta, ingenuo e infelice;
ora il mio cuore non è capace, in questa lieta
stagione, che di cattiveria, di crudeltà, perché
smarrita è la via del domani,
viene solo la notte e il triste vento. E
del dolore l'eco più assordante
è che non venga risarcito – mai.
È secco ormai il mio seme, spento e atroce
– basta mettersene un po' in bocca e sentire
il suo sapore di morte – per quanto ancora
corra lento o veloce sul ventre bianco
dei sani e indifesi ragazzi.
Limitato e feroce questo tempo
ha strangolato la mia unica grazia;
di non essere nato a nessuna nascita,
incolpevole e idiota.

the tender and moronic rites, of incontinence
and easy erections, of bitter semen
to gag on quickly or not,
depending on what trick is lurking about,
or the cross-dressed police stalking, old
fairy of the Hospice for the elderly in search of some
blond or dark-haired boy, brutal and rugged,
escaped from the Inferno of Reform School
and fallen into this other Inferno, less thuggish
for sure, but more desolate, where solitude
more shockingly alone, of the soul
and the body, possesses you entirely, never numb
to the hopefulness of a chance encounter.

Here, everything, Coliseum, is in the service of the erection
and damn the fool who for the first time dares
to force kisses on the mouth, along with all these
exhausting ejaculates, it will be his first and last.
But why do I look for something here I will never find?
For what self-flagellating, inexorable mystery?
Here, within you, even returning as a boy, I don't return
as a boy, as I once did, ingenuous and unhappy;
now my heart no longer capable, in this happy
season, which because of evil and cruelty
has lost the way to tomorrow,
only nighttime and the desolate wind comes. And
of the pain the most deafening echo
is that it will never be redeemed—ever.
By now my semen is dried out, heinous and spent
—just putting a bit in your mouth gives you a sense
of its death—for as long as it still
flows slowly or quickly on the white stomachs
of the healthy and defenseless boys.
These times are limited and ferocious
they've strangled my only grace;
of not being birthed from any
idiotic or guiltless womb.

Aspetterò la notte, lunga notte a chi conta
le prime, acerbe erezioni nel seme latteo
o grigiastro delle lunghe masturbazioni,
le lunghe notti e il triste vento, sapiente
che s'insinua fra cunicoli e sterri, ferendo
l'odore magro, acido dell'orina abbondante
e festosa dei ragazzotti, bassi e tarchiati,
di una periferia immensa che come una
trappola circonda la viziosa Roma.
Vento lieto se scombina i ricordi
anonimi di un'anonima, effimera gioventù
senza tregua vissuta per questo approdo infame,
fra le maestose rovine di un vecchio, disamorato
monumento ormai in pensione e funestato,
ogni tanto da qualche disoccupato con mogli
e tre figli a carico, che all'improvviso
si butta giù, dalle stelle, sul selciato.

Ti lascio, Colosseo, alla tua prolungata
nei secoli agonia senza armonia tranne
qualche festosa voce di ragazzo o di marinaio
in congedo limitato. Ti lascio al tuo tetro sonno,
da cui ti risveglierai forse ad un altro,
meno servile, secolo.

I will wait for the night, the long night for those whose
first, unripe erections matter in the milky
or grayish semen of lengthy masturbations,
the long nights and the knowing gloomy wind,
that flows through tunnels and excavations, mitigating
the thin, acidic odor of the abundant
and celebratory urine of these short and stocky, butch boys
from the immense suburbs that, as a noose
surrounds this overindulged Roma.
Sweet wind if it unsettles these anonymous memories
of an anonymous, ephemeral adolescence
lived without respite for this infamous landing place,
among the majestic ruins of this old unloved
monument by now funereal and desecrated
every so often, by some unemployed man with his wife
and three children in tow, who suddenly,
throws himself down, from the stars, onto the pavement.

I leave you Coliseum, to your prolonged
centuries-long agony without harmony except
for some festive voice of a boy or a sailor
on weekend leave. I leave you to your bleak sleep,
from which you may reawaken in some other,
less servile, century.

L'avversario (1994)

The Adversary

I

Né pipistrelli né serpi
mangerei nell'Aldilà normale
dei ladri; né ripensandoci
potrei farlo se il culmine
della Fine, il gran Finale
fosse mangiare me stesso
o quel che rimane di me stesso.
Ad ognuno il suo pranzo
più o meno ecologico, senza
sputare nel piatto dei digiuni.

]

I would eat neither bats
nor snakes in the Otherworldly
every day of thieves; nor in reconsidering
could I if the culmination
of the End, the grand Finale
consisted in devouring myself entirely
or what remains of me.
To each his own meal
more or less eco-friendly, without
spitting in the plate of the starved.

II

Legge di natura lo schiaffo
tradizionale; il bacio
e la mano incerta
– il singhiozzo della creatura –
grido: mi lasciasti, anima mia
mi lasciasti, nel vento
te ne sei andato, non tornerai.
E fuoriesce, s'invertigina
la vita passata e ne muore.

II

This traditional blow
is natural law; a kiss
and an uncertain hand
—a creature's hiccup—
I cry: you abandoned me, my soul
you abandoned me, in the wind
you left, you'll not return.
And the past life pours out,
woozily and dies there.

III (ROMA 1989)

È avventizio il mio essere reale.
Sleale è insistere su chi sono io.
Il punto di partenza è scontato –
l'arrivo è certo nello stato
attuale: morte come sostanza
o strato finale di un cuore malato.

Oh, vorrei rinascere, ritornare indietro
ma non posso. Troppo ho peccato
di peccati non miei, attribuiti
a posteri, mancati inganni.
Cerco amori nuovi, violente sere.
Perdono chiedo a chi non amai.
Forse verrò domani ad un prato
verde, – e non sarò più solo.

III (Rome 1989)

My being real is makeshift.
It's faithless to insist on who I am.
The point of departure is taken for granted—
arrival is certain in its present
state: death as sustenance
or final barrier of a feeble heart.

Oh, I would like to be reborn, turn back
but I cannot. I've sinned too many
sins not my own, attributed
a posteriori, missed deceptions.
I'm looking for new loves, violent nights.
I ask forgiveness to those I did not love.
Perhaps tomorrow I'll come to a green
field,—and I'll no longer be alone.

VIII

Il sonno è una piccola morte
richiede commossa pazienza –
attenderlo è sperare
in una resurrezione antica:

io aspetto la morte
per dormire poche ore
nel caldo di un letto
intrecciato ad un corpo
infelice e sterile, il mio:
non siamo eterni
e questo cadavere intrigante
presto supereremo.

VIII

Sleep is a small death
that requires fretful patience—
to wait for it is to hope
for an ancient resurrection.

I wait for death
to sleep a few hours
in the warmth of a bed
intertwined with an unhappy
and sterile body, mine:
we are not eternal
and we will soon overcome
this intriguing cadaver.

L'AVVERSARIO

Non furono immagini, raggianti e regali
immagini del reale salutare il mio forte:
il forte di ogni ora rimescolata, nella
siesta o controra delle brame assolute.
E trascorsi i secoli in ghingheri
trasecolammo con scheletri tardivi di Musa
antiquata lungo le cime dei monti Tiburtini
invano cercati da mani infantili.
Non cercammo i cuori lacerati e indecisi
né il lieto sapore dei muscoli d'Acciaio.

Sì, immagini, rumori: mai il mio forte,
il vero forte, o panforte della poesia –
truccata idea dei sensi inquieti
o calpestati singhiozzi nel letto
ospite e ospitale, orinale mentre tendo
l'orecchio alla salita delle scale,
le mani collegiali chiuse e derise
dentro la palma umida, liquida,
vivendo al capestro le sensazioni
virginali.

Stanze illuminate, poi. Garbate
ingiurie del vino, ma il giorno è
passato ormai, orfano innamorato
agitandomi in piedi, in ansia: apro
la finestra nel freddo lunare
spio la mortalità terrestre e serale:
tombale silenzio, e noia, noia
calamità naturale del poco amarsi
nel riaccendere la luce
perché svaniscano gli incerti fantasmi
della notte.

The Adversary

They weren't radiant and regal images,
images of royal greetings my strength:
the stronghold of every hour reshuffled, in
a nap or the limitless cravings of summer afternoons.
And having enjoyed centuries of pageantry
we were dumbstruck by sluggish skeletons of an antiquated
Muse along the summits of the Tiburtini mountains
uselessly searched for with childlike hands.
We weren't looking for battered tentative hearts
nor the happy taste of muscles of Steel.

Yes, images, noise: never my strength
my true strength, or my sweet nougat of poetry—
the dressed-up idea of disordered senses
or muffled sighs in a hospitable
guest bed, urinal while I strain
to listen in the hallway stairwell,
the youthful tight-fisted scorned
hands, wet in sweaty palms,
living these virginal sensations
as if in a noose.

Afterward, luminous rooms. Polite
insults of wine, but the day has
passed by now, beloved orphan
stirring me to my feet, anxiously, I open
the window to the moonlit cold
I spy earthly and nightly mortality:
a tomblike silence, and boredom, boredom
the natural calamity of minimal self-love
while turning the light on again
so these uncertain phantasms of the night
may disappear.

In Calabria

Davanti immacolate montagne
nel sole meridiano indicano
al viandante la sosta e la calma.
Ma fino a quando? E io chi sono
se ancora ardo di voluttà segreta
nel giorno finito, anzi nei giorni
finiti del mondo caduto?

La casa è decrepita
come piace a me, ma troppo tardi,
mi dico, è arrivata, come tutto
ormai tardi è arrivato agli umani.
Panni stesi al balcone al vento
del Pollino, letti disfatti, aurore
così si placa nel risentimento
la vita che ci è data vivere.
Il mio io è distrutto non esiste:
la realtà è un nome assiderato. Il mio
io non c'è – è merda d'uccello a volo
sulle case dai tetti sconnessi
dove la pioggia suona il suo ritmo
incalzante nella notte scura di luna.
La leopardiana natura
ancora esiste e insiste per poco,
mi prega di non sprecarla con lo sguardo
ossessionato da vacanze blasfeme,
perdoni e incastri silenziosi
di memorie austere, prigioniere
di fiati industriali, di chimere inquinanti
di forsennata plastica portata
da famiglie impotenti per lussuriosi
figli con l'orecchino d'oro
e la catenina ubriaca.

In Calabria

The immaculate mountains
in the southern sun before us offer
a calming respite for the wanderer.
But until when? And who am I
if I still burn with secret lust
at day's end, or in the final
days of a fallen world?

The house is ramshackle
as I like it, but much too late,
I tell myself, like everything
that's arrived too late for humanity.
Clothes hang on the balcony in the wind
of the Pollino, unmade beds, dawns
that's how the life that's given us
to live is placated in resentment.
My I is destroyed it's nonexistent:
reality is a name frozen in time. My
I isn't here—it's bird shit flying
onto houses of lop-sided roofs
where rain sounds its urgent rhythm
in dark moonlit nights.
Leopardian nature
still exists and insists for a little,
it begs me not to waste her on a gaze
obsessed with blasphemous diversions,
pardons and silent incriminations
of stark memories, prisoner
of industrial breaths, of polluted chimeras
of ridiculous amounts of plastic brought
by helpless families for their lascivious
sons who wear a golden earring
and jangly necklace.

Forse un tempo credevo a Dio:
vivevo in eterno il giovane
corpo, il breve corpo della gioventù
del mondo ora malato di plastica
suicida e omicida, nel ghetto
dei pensieri tutti uguali della massa
che vuole scongiuro e disamore,
odio e portate al ristorante
di plastica atomica per eroina
digiuna. Oggi è a me, inetto
indagatore di disperate speranze
giovanili che faccio guerra, non
cambiando la fine della vita
in rinascita perenne. Mi faccio
guerra senza sapere il male.

O Dio di latta, ogni qualvolta
ti penso, tu esisti. Io penso
trovarti, illuso!, in una chiesa
di cemento o acqua ragia.
Devo dunque convertirmi, baciare
la terra manipolata e avvelenata,
seguire su una montagna di Pollino
una vecchia centenaria di Crosia
che si chiude in una tomba di cemento
e svaria nel bunker la sua assenza
di psicologia: un garage l'accoglie
non un fico o un ulivo millenario,
e così si ritempra al calore dell'estate
incipiente che mi toglie le forze
poche del domani antico.
Morire per lei, per la terra, sarà
facile disguido, facile avventura:
per me, ostile terrore ladro, paura.

Perhaps once I believed in God:
I lived eternally in the youthful
body, the brief body of youth
in a world now sick with plastic
suicide and homicides, in the ghetto
of the masses' same thoughts
that want superstition and discord,
hatred and outings to the restaurant
of nuclear plastic to withdraw from
heroin. Today it's my turn, inept
prober of desperate youthful
expectations who makes war, without
changing the ending into perennial
rebirth. I wage war on myself
without knowing its evil effects.

O tin can God, whenever
I think of you, you exist. I think
of finding you, deluded!, in a cement
or whitewashed church.
I must therefore convert, kiss
the manhandled and poisoned earth
follow up a mountain of the Pollino
a hundred-year-old woman from Crosia
who shuts herself in a cement tomb
where she pours her psychological lack
into a bunker: a garage welcomes her
not a fig tree or a millennial olive tree,
and in that way she adjusts to the incipient heat
of summer that strips me of my minimal
strength for an ancient tomorrow.
To die for her, for this earth, would be
an easy mistake, an agreeable adventure;
for me, hostile terrorized thief, fear.

L'OMBRELLO DI ELSA

L'ombrello di Elsa è un eroe
che cavalca le tempeste del cuore
un'aquila che sfida le tristi
giornate.
L'ombrello di Elsa
fugge il sereno s'avventa
sull'umido piovoso inverno
della vita caduta, nella primavera
impacciata s'avventura per mano.

Canta le mestizie dell'estate
al suo colmo quando agosto rompe
la stagione calda con le piogge
e il sole mescolati
smisurati da un settembre agli inizi.

Allora vibro all'unisono
col mare in burrasca, settembre
è il mio mese; il Leone il segno
di Elsa, che mi vuole sempre
accanto, la nascita
è lontana, la vita ormai mi guarda
col sapore della fine prossima
e ne tremo.

Allevare la morte è impresa difficile
per chi è ricacciato nella dura
dimensione di un ombrello.

ELSA'S UMBRELLA

Elsa's umbrella is a hero
who charges through storms of the heart
an eagle who defies sorrowful
days.
Elsa's umbrella
evades serenity hurling
against the damp rainy winter
of a fallen life that in spring
clumsily takes adventure in hand.

It sings the melancholy of summer
to its brim when August snaps
the hot spell with rains
mixed with sun made
boundless by the beginning of September.

Then I resound in unison
with the raging sea, September
is my month; the Lion
Elsa's sign, who always wants me
near, birth
is faraway, life by now watches me
with the taste of an imminent end
and I shudder.

To raise the dead is a difficult task
for those who are thrust beneath the umbrella's
grave expanse.

Ieri un famoso libro mi tenne compagnia;
oggi, due luglio, una strana pioggia estiva
lava le sporche case di via de' Pettinari,
ed io aspetto dopo aver pulito il cesso
nell'afa romana, sudando, pregando
nella casa dove ormai vivo da vent'anni
e qualcuno, uccello di malaugurio,
ha profetato che ne uscirà morto –
meglio lasciarla molto prima, sì, in fretta:

I gatti non ci sono più, l'odore
è rimasto; nel cielo nuvole strane
annunciano il temporale oltre la pioggia –
è stata finora fitta e silenziosa

Chi ama pensa al destino immenso
alla privazione di tutte le libertà.
Forse non verrai, l'acqua ti fermò
dentro un bar dove drogate fanciulle
ti porteranno in salvo, ad una riva remota.

Io, sempre io – finto io – calmo
leggo le righe del nostro aspro esilio.

Ma se anche tu più bello venissi a me
uguale ti vorrei a come eri
se più bello venissi e più leggiadro
uguale ti vorrei a come eri, modesto
negli occhi e con le piaghe sulla bocca
minuta da baciare.
O bocca strepitosa non invecchiare
l'anima di chi ti bacia!

Yesterday a famous book kept me company;
today, July 2, a strange summer rain
washes the dirty houses of via de' Pettinari,
and I wait after having cleaned the toilet
in the Roman sultriness, sweating, praying
in the house where by now I've lived twenty years
and someone, a bird of evil omen,
has prophesized that I will leave here dead—
better to leave here sooner then, yes, in a hurry:

The cats are no longer here, the smell
lingers; in the sky strange clouds
presage a storm beyond the rain—
until now thick and silent

He who loves thinks about an immense destiny
about the privation of all liberties.
Perhaps you won't come, the rain stopped you
in a bar where drugged girls
will lead you rescued, to a remote shore.

I always I—a fake me—calmly
read the lines of our bitter exile.

But even if you came to me handsomer
I'd want you as you were
if you came more beautiful and more graceful
I'd still want you as you were, with shy
eyes and sores on your tiny
kissable mouth.
O fabulous mouth don't age
the soul who kisses you!

Ma se vieni ancora né bello né brutto
Non vieni, non vieni, nella casa del peccato,
come se tu non fossi più, come dimenticato.

Più che morto non sei, più di morire non si può,
ma ancora non sei morto, no? e allora perché
non vieni, né bello né brutto come sei,
come venivi una volta abbracciato alla carne
t'accetterei ugualmente anche tossico spento
con gli occhi ciechi, dove sei, perché non viene?
Dove ti sei fermato? Perché non vieni, non vieni
come? Pallido sei? Brutto o bello vieni, vieni
basta che io non credo che tu non sei. Più.

But if you return neither handsome nor ugly
Don't come, don't return, to the house of sin,
as if you no longer existed, as if forgotten.

You are not greater than death, one cannot do more than die,
but still you aren't dead, right? then why
don't you return, neither beautiful nor ugly as you are,
as you used to come once clinging to flesh,
I'd accept you just the same even as a wasted drug addict
with blind eyes, where are you, why don't you come?
Where have you stopped? Why don't you come, you don't
why? You're pale? Ugly or beautiful come, come back
as long as I don't believe you no longer exist. Ever.

Scaricato alla stazione di Martina Franca
fra trulli autunnali e polverosi fichi d'India
riversi sul suolo arso di mia Puglia materna –
abbandonato alle fredde rotaie di un treno per Bari
livido di una rabbia mattutina
ho pregato il Dio feroce degli esuli

L'esilio comincia dove finisce la terra
sacra degli amanti perpetui oltre la morte
dove il cuore impazzito sale le scale della sorte

Dio della velocità ferma dell'attimo fuggente
rapiscimi in una notte senza fondo
dove l'addio consumato fra pallide lenzuola
nasconda l'ulteriore figlio sconsacrato.

Cast-off at the station in Martina Franca
among autumnal stone huts and dusty prickly pear
heaped on the scorched ground of my maternal Puglia—
abandoned to the cold train tracks toward Bari
livid with a daily rage
I prayed to the ferocious God of exiles

Exile begins where the sacred land
of perpetual lovers ends beyond death
where the crazed heart climbs fate's stairs

God of stopped time in a fleeting moment
ravage me in a night without end
where a farewell consumed among worn sheets
conceals the next desecrated son.

GATTI

Siete miei prigionieri
prigionieri dell'amore dunque
anche il tetto vi è proibito
per ragioni di forza maggiore
e la vostra vita passa e ripassa
in due sole stanzette umide
dove vi rinchiudo quando esco
per serate di gala sinistra

Io sono vostro prigioniero
prigioniero di tutto
anche dell'aria che respiro
o dell'abiezione raggiunta
in liberi orgasmi di sventura.
Non voglio giocare più.
Non sono Leopardi orami,
e neppure Kavafis. Chi sono
dunque? La domanda è pertinente
più di ogni risposta evasiva
o paradossale ("un poeta" =
"un buffone") alla quale
si può obiettare certo
che il nulla e il tutto
sono la stessissima cosa −
gatti amorosi permettendo,
e, a contrario dei gatti,
in natura i poeti
non esistono.

Cats

You are my prisoners
prisoners of love therefore
for you even the roof is prohibited
for reasons of higher powers
and your lives pass by and pass again
in two solitary damp rooms
where I lock you in when I leave
for my nights of sinister galas

I am your prisoner
prisoner of everything
even the air I breathe
or of the abjection I encounter
during liberal orgasms of misadventure.
I don't want to play anymore.
I'm not Leopardi after all,
nor Cavafy. Who am I
then? The question is relevant
more than any evasive
or paradoxical answer ("a poet" =
"a buffoon") about whom
one could certainly object
since nothingness and everything
are exactly the same—
excluding the beloved cats,
and, in contrast to cats,
in nature poets
don't exist.

Proclama sul fascino (1996)

Proclamation on Glamour

Il fascino

L'arcano fascino dell'amore tradito
che fa tremare il sogno e l'incubo
e poi si avvera, s'incista in maniera
che un'anima perduta, di sera,
tocca con mano alata il goloso,
sospirato tradimento, incerto e vero:
il tradimento del tradito, aspettiamo!
Qualcuno invece, mortificante osanna
dirà: Che fascino ha il tradimento?
Non è più affascinante e gaglioffo
virtuoso e immondo un amore felice?
Ma chi tremerà come trema il mondo
se non sente il fascino della persona
amata, non la rincuora e se esce di casa,
sale in macchina, in autobus, in taxi
e va all'appuntamento, al delirio
del destino innamorato che può morte
pretendere o vita presente, sangue,
ma sempre ti esclude, ti annienta
solidale nel silenzio dei sensi.
Cambiamo immagini al fascino
del poeta allora: se l'innamorato
è fedele? La fedeltà non esiste
dirà l'avvocato del Diavolo,
la Sfinge a tre Teste, l'Orrore Brutto, e
allora pensate ai pochi attimi di tempo,
ore, minuti, secondi forse che vi concede
la persona amata, che per voi ha fascino:
in un letto a palpitare di lussuria:
così circondata da un'aureola, come fosse
una luce di santità la seguite con gli occhi
della memoria, la rimpiangete, la perdonate,
la baciate sulle labbra fredde e intrise

GLAMOUR

The mysterious glamour of betrayed love
that makes sleep and nightmare restless
and then real, embeds in such a way
at night, that a lost soul actually
touches this greedy, lifelike and longed-for
betrayal, with an outstretched hand:
we come to expect this betrayal of the betrayed!
Someone else however, mortified exclaims:
What's so glamorous about betrayal?
Isn't a happy love more fascinating
and good-for-nothing, righteous and immoral?
But who will tremble as the world trembles
if they don't feel the fascination of a beloved,
if they don't feel emboldened to leave the house,
ride in the car, the bus, the taxi
and go to the appointment, toward the delirium
of an enamored destiny that can pretend
to be deadly or provide life, blood,
but will always exclude you, annihilate you
agreeably in the silence of your feelings.
Let's switch images then to the glamour
of the poet: if the beloved
is faithful? Fidelity doesn't exist
the lawyer of the Devil, the Three-headed
Sphinx, and Brutal Horror will say,
therefore think about the brief moments,
hours, minutes, seconds perhaps the beloved
concedes that for you hold fascination:
in a bed pulsating with lust:
surrounded by a halo, as if it were
a saintly light you follow with memory's
hindsight, which you regret, you forgive,
and kiss on its cold lips soaked

di tradimento. La verità è che tradire
ha fascino, violento e incorruttibile,
e i traditori andrebbero puniti, marchiati
a sangue, bruciati vivi, sulla pubblica piazza!

Una morte lenta legata alla gelosia
dell'amante che non sa darsi pace,
e alla fine propone, invece del sangue
purificatore e smentito, un viaggio!

Ecco, ecco nel viaggio il Fascino
aumenta, ritorna sublime, nel viaggio
tutto si sublima, si canta, si balla,
e la persona amata vi guarda, beata
mentre si vola, o in treno, o in nave
si fugge verso le isole Felici o il Paradiso.
Allora sarete in Paradiso, e chi può dire
che lì tutti, compreso Dio, non abbiamo fascino?

in betrayal. The truth is betrayal
is fascinating, violent and incorruptible,
and traitors will be punished, marked
in blood, burned alive, in a public square!

A slow death bound to the jealousy
of a lover who doesn't know how to find peace,
and in the end proposes flight, instead
of a purifying and disavowed bloodline!

Here, here, during the journey Glamour
is heightened, it returns sublime, during the journey
everything becomes sublime, we sing, we dance,
and the beloved looks at you, blessed
while in flight, or when fleeing by train, or by boat
toward the Blissful Islands or to Paradise.
Then you will be in Paradise, and who can say,
that there everyone, including God, isn't glamorous?

Marilyn

Marilyn, Marilina, come una canzone
marinera Marilina se ne andò all'alba,
uscì dalla favola stupida che fu la sua vita.
Qualcuno si ricorda una foto di lei,
povera creatura ignorante, anzi di te,
mia bionda sorellina senza pace ormai
con Carson McCullers, Karen Blixen
le streghe sono tornate! Fuggiamo
dall'intelligenza, e in più c'è Miller
Arthur il tuo pigmalione feroce
Arturo come Rimbaud dalle suole
volanti, no, nemmeno a parlarne,
un borghese meno capace di reggere
il confronto con la tua follia
di sorellina stupida e innocente
che vuole stare con le scrittrici,
gli intellettuali. Che noia!
Sperando che resti sempre Marilina,
Marilyn, bionda sorellina, oca
giuliva purtroppo con la nevrosi
giusta. Qualcuno un cantastorie
di favole apocalittiche
dovrebbe cantare il modo
in cui partisti dal mondo dei vivi!
Delitto o suicido, ma sempre Venere
in agguato a punirti, e al cui capriccio
tutto il tuo sangue ancora si ravviva
dopo la morte alata e non cercata,
e invaghirsi di te è un mistero
testamento e leggenda di spaesati
di vigliacchi untori dell'eros
la tua calda voce di sorellina,
la tua sostanza è impalpabile

MARILYN

Marilyn, Marilina, like a mariner's song
Marilina, has disappeared with the dawn,
she's escaped the stupid fairytale that was her life.
Someone remembers a photo of her,
sad innocent creature, a photo of you I mean,
my blonde restless sister along with
Carson McCullers, Karen Blixen now
the haunting has returned! We've
gone beyond intelligibility, and there's Miller
Arthur your first ferocious Pygmalion
Arthur as in Rimbaud of the fleeing
soles, no, not even worth talking about,
a bourgeois unable to handle
or confront your madness
as a silly innocent sister
who wants to hang out with writers,
with intellectuals. What a drag!
I wish you could always be Marilina,
Marilyn, a blonde little sister, silly
goose with a righteous neurosis.
Some troubadour
of apocalyptic fairytales
should sing about how
you departed from the world of the living!
Crime or suicide, Venus always
in ambush ready to hurt you, to whose whim
all your blood still revives
after a winged and unsought death,
and our beguilement of you is a mystery
testament and legend of the bewildered
of the sleazy cowards of eroticism
your sexy sister voice,
your impalpable being

ormai, rende concrete gioie serene
della nostra generazione perduta
che ti amò, mitica, o anche prima
come ballerina, certo una bambola
di carne, non ha letto Freud,
per fortuna può far più male che bene,
ma tu volevi difenderti, o forse
esistere oltre l'apparenza
del tuo corpo muliebre e immortale
nella sua mortalità lasciato ai corvi,
ai nani, ai masturbatori solitari,
nel ricordo di chi ti vede;
vecchi bavosi e frustati.
Ci volevano nervi più saldi,
e tu non l'hai avuti per resistere
alla sfida del tempo. Per questo
ci piaci: perché fosti
una vittima, una sconfitta
dal tempo e dalla storia infausta
dei nostri giorni peccatori.

by now, offers concrete and serene
joy to our lost generation
that loved you, mythically, or even earlier
as a dancer, undeniably a doll
of flesh, who hadn't read Freud,
thank goodness since it can do more harm than good,
but you wanted to defend yourself, or perhaps
to exist beyond the appearance
of your womanly and immortal body
in its mortality left to crows,
to dwarves, and to solitary masturbators,
to the memory of those who see you;
slobbering frustrated old fools.
We needed more steeled nerves,
and you didn't have them to endure
the challenges of the day. For this
we love you: because you were
a victim, a conquest
of the times and of our ominous history
of our sinful days.

Traditore, menagramo, sporificante assedio
dei tuoi sensi inesistenti, come ti detesto!
Contravvenendo al vangelo dei giusti che rinnego
per te rinnegato che offendi la Scrittura, ma
non è la mia anima piena del Tutto che ti odia,
bensì qualcosa in me che chiamo Ragione;
le parti basse affievolite dal sonno
premono per spremere la linfa vitale
che in te non arriva mai al cielo dei Rimorsi.
Il tuo prossimo libro: piange la tua carne
bastonata dall'omicidio commesso
sul tuo rozzo corpo di provinciale malspeso.
Tu hai sporcato poesia, sporcherai anche morte!

Traitor, mishap, filthy besieger
of your inexistent senses, how I detest you!
Transgressing the Gospel of the just that I repudiate
for you renegade who offends Scripture, though
it's not my soul full of Everything that hates you,
but rather something in me called Reason;
the base parts depleted by sleep
pressure me to squeeze the vital lymph
that in you never arrives to the heaven of Regrets.
Your next book: cries your flesh
thrashed by the murder enacted
on your crass body of a dissipated provincial.
You've dishonored poetry, you'll dishonor even death!

Laggiù, oltre il telefono,
riposi in un letto matrimoniale
aspetti la sposa vera, la spirale
tratterà i dovuti suicidi.
Aspirare l'inverno o il vento
battendo sugli infissi d'alluminio
non c'è speranza oltre i secoli bui
del martirio. Attendo
il tuo corpo, l'anima è volata via.

Down there, beyond the telephone,
you rest in a matrimonial bed
and wait for the true bride, the gyre
handles purported suicides.
Inhaling winter or wind
as it beats on aluminum panes
there's no hope beyond dark centuries
of martyrdom. I await
your body, the soul has flown away.

Sei Dio forse
solo perché t'ho amato
e ora inguaribile
ritorno a te
bestemmia, insulto
emblema casto del Passato.

You are God perhaps
solely because I've loved you
and now incurable
I return to you
blasphemy, insult
chaste emblem of the Past.

Ora, tra i morti, mio libero fratello
tra i morti di un lontano cimitero
sarai di sudore vuoto e di sangue
freddo solo del calore della terra;

se batterà d'estate ancora il sole
calmo nel cielo senza nuvole
e il pianto dell'amante resterà
secco fissato sulla guancia asciutta

indistinto amore ti poterà fra i venti
alla distruzione. E il nulla ti sarà
compagno fedelissimo e insaziato.

Now, among the dead, my liberated brother
among the dead of a distant cemetery
you'll exist empty of sweat and cold-
blooded alone in the heat of earth

if the sun once again scalds in summer
calmly in a sky without clouds
and the lover's tears remain
static fixed on a dry cheek

dispassionately love will carry you among the winds
of destruction. And nothingness will
be your faithful and insatiable friend.

Saresti morto di AIDS
poeta assassinato
se fossi ancora restato
fra i vivi incerti

che ti piange è perduto
al ricordo e al passato.

You would be dead of AIDS
murdered poet
if you'd still remained
among the uncertain living

whomever mourns you is lost
to memory and to the past.

Congedo

I critici ostili li ho amati invano.
Ora il Buddismo me li tiene lontani.
Dio mi assolva i peccati letterari.
Quelli sessuali non son né tali
né osceni reati da prigione, lager
o manicomio. Se sono un expoeta è
solo colpa mia. I critici li perdono.

Farewell

I have loved hostile critics in vain.
Now Buddhism keeps them far away from me.
God will absolve my literary sins.
Those sexual ones are neither so many
nor obscene crimes worthy of prison, lager,
or insane asylum. If I'm a failed poet it's
my own fault. I forgive the critics.

Di nuovo ecco la ripetizione:
non so a chi potrà interessare, detto
in prosa, dopo aver fornicato con pentole
e fornelli. Sono diventato un perfetto
casalingo, chiuso in casa, sognando
Dio o il misticismo. Scorro le novità
librarie: Teresa d'Avila, San Giovanni
della Croce: ma la mia croce qual è?
I gatti ridono sornioni, dentro
una cassetta, la loro casetta:
i giochi di parole mi stuccano, le rime
mi inquietano come muse spente e annegate:
la vita passa davanti alla stufa
di ghisa, eroina delle mie giornate.
Non so abbandonarmi al flusso del tempo:
la poesia è tutta digerita. Fuori
febbraio annuncia primavera;
partirò per la Sicilia, la Poesia
resterà unica padrona di Roma.
Telefonando avrò notizie,
scongiurerò eventi, crescite e rinascite,
sempre di meno in questo mondo infetto.

Once again behold repetition:
I don't know whom it will interest, told
prosaically, after having fornicated with anything
that moves. I've become a perfect
househusband, locked inside, dreaming
of God and mysticism. I browse bookstore
novelties: Teresa of Avila, Saint John
of the Cross: but which cross is mine?
The cats laugh craftily, within
a little drawer, their drawer house:
puns silence me like plaster, rhymes
unnerve me like spent and drowned muses:
life passes in front of a cast-iron stove
heroine of my days.
I don't know how to trust the flux of time:
poetry has been ravaged. Outside
February announces the spring;
I'll depart for Sicily, Poetry
remains the sole overseer of Rome.
Phoning I'll get some news,
I'll forestall events, births and rebirths
always fewer in this infected world.

Acknowledgments

Thank you to the following editors and journals where my translations of Dario Bellezza's poems were previously published, sometimes in slightly varying versions:

Atlanta Review: "To Pier Paolo Pasolini" and "[I listened to death in my dream]"

Arkansas International: "My House the Entryway" and "Practical Activities"

Asymptote: Tenth Anniversary Issue: "[And I abandon death. Plaything of God]," "[In my night the worst of your mornings]," "[You no longer enter into my unraveled life]," and "[Where you sleep I watch over]"

Colorado Review: "To Hart Crane," "Serpenta," and *from* "Praise for the Male Body," "[Neither male nor female, that gaze]" and "[Hey boy down there, hidden treasure]"

Interim: "To Elsa Morante" and "Coliseum"

NEA website: "[Infant of a slightly precocious infancy]"

2Bridges Review: "[Good-bye hearts, good-bye loved ones]" and "[From the other room you masturbate without praise]"

Witness: "Glamour" and six poems *from* "Nothingness" "[Traitor, mishap, filthy besieger]," "[Down there, beyond the telephone]," "[You are God perhaps]," "[Now, among the dead, my liberated brother]" "[You would be dead of AIDS]"

Words Without Borders: "[Cast-off at the station in Martina Franca]" and "The City and the Writer" (poem and essay about Bellezza's influence and the writing scene in Rome, Italy)

Translated poems also appeared in the following anthology:

Wayne Miller and Kevin Prufer, eds., *Modern European Poets (1968–2008)* (Minneapolis: Graywolf, 2008): "[I believe I should have a child]" and "[I licked you between dirty sheets]" (I coedited the Italian section and provided translations of nine poems with biographical notes).

Infinite gratitude to poet-translator Geoffrey Brock for choosing this book for the Wisconsin Prize for Poetry in Translation and for all you've achieved on behalf of Italian and world poetry through your important work. Abundant gratitude to Sean Bishop and Jesse Lee Kercheval for their dedicated efforts on behalf of the University of Wisconsin Press and for their kindness in putting this book forward. Special thanks also to the director and uber professional, hardworking colleagues at the University of Wisconsin Press, above all, Dennis Lloyd, Jacqueline Krass, Alison Shay, Jessica Hasan, and Jennifer Conn and their design team.

Thank you also to the village-*villaggio-paese* of friends and organizations who sustained me as I was writing and researching and rewriting this translation project—especially Caterina Romeo and Edvige Giunta for offering expert advice on endless questions; for offering convivial conversation and consistently delicious food and shared affection. To Tim Cavanaugh, my partner, for his abundant and chaotic love, always good-natured daily energy, and his answering of endless questions about what sounds better in English!

To Anthony Tamburri, my first graduate-level Italian professor and mentor. To Francesca Borrione for the many conversations puzzling over poems; gratitude to Nathalie Handal for her tender loving care, and guidance with the introduction; gratitude also for an always-supportive friend through the years, Patricia Spears Jones. To my cousin Franco Di Stefano, who found and gifted me a treasured first edition of Dario Bellezza's *Morte segreta* (1976) and set all this energy into another gear. To my cousin Marco Di Stefano; and to my beloved cousin Beatrice (Bice) Todisco, and Nello Vescovi for their unwavering support and artistic sensibilities. Special thanks also to my extended family of Italian friends: Francesco, Cristina, Maria Teresa, Antonella, Giulio, Salva, Maddalena, and Maria.

For Hollis Kurman, my polyglot dear friend who understands all the in-betweens of our shared languages. For Mary Giaimo dear friend and editor, for the free editing and copyediting lessons. To Stanislao Pugliese for his faith in this project and his guidance. And, of course, gratitude to my students and colleagues at the University of Rhode Island, especially Martha Rojas and Mary Cappello.

I'm also especially grateful to the University of Rhode Island College of Arts and Sciences and the Center of the Humanities for their fellowship support. To the National Endowment of the Arts for a Translation Fellowship; to the Richmond American International University of London, Rome Programme, the Nida Translation Institute, the American Academy in Rome, and La Macina, San Cresci for related fellowships and residencies and the gift of time in some of the most beautiful locales imaginable. Special thanks to Anna Borrelli and Luisa Rovetta at Grandi & Associati for helping to shepherd my work with the Bellezza family.

Finally, some more friends, colleagues, and family to thank—who offered and/or continue to offer inspiration along the way of this journey: especially dear Joanna Clapps Herman, Carrie Tocci, Donald Revell, Claudia Keelan, Ryan Calabretta-Sajder, Alan Gravano, Colleen Ryan, Jackie Osherow, Parneshia Jones, Derek Pollard, Luca Baldoni, Becka McKay; my sisters Josephine and Laura; my niece Cesira; and my recently departed mother, Stella Todisco Covino, and everyone else I may be forgetting. I hope to celebrate with you a few decades more. Grazie infinite.

Bibliography

Poetry Books by Dario Bellezza (selected)

Invettive e licenze. Milan: Garzanti, 1971.
Morte segreta. Milan: Garzanti, 1976.
Libro d'amore. Parma: Guanda, 1982. 2nd ed., 1992.
Io. Mondadori: Milan: Mondadori, 1983.
Colosseo—Apologia di Teatro. Catania: Pellicanolibri, 1985.
Serpenta. Milan: Mondadori, 1987.
Libro di poesia. Milan: Garzanti, 1992.
L'avversario. Milan: Mondadori, 1996.
Proclama sul fascino. Milan: Mondadori, 1996.
Poesie 1971–1996. Edited by Elio Pecora. Milan: Mondadori, 2002.
Tutte le poesie. Edited by Roberto Deidier. Milan: Mondadori, 2015.

Prose, Theater, and Translations by Dario Bellezza (selected)

Georges Bataille, Simona. Rome: L'airone, 1969.
Arthur Rimbaud, Poesie. Milan: Garzanti, 1977.
L'innocenza. Bari: De Donato, 1970.
Lettere da Sodoma. Milan: Garzanti, 1972.
Il carnefice. Milan: Garzanti, 1973.
Angelo. Milan: Garzanti, 1979.
Turbamento. Milan: Mondadori, 1984.
Morte di Pasolini. Milan: Mondadori, 1986.
L'amore felice. Milan: Rusconi,1986.
Testamento di sangue. Milan: Garzanti, 1992.
Nozze col diavolo. Venice: Marsilio, 1995.

Il poeta assassinato: Una riflessione, un'ipotesi, una sfida sulla morte di Pier Paolo Pasolini. Venice: Gli specchi, Marsilio, 1996.

Pier Paolo Pasolini. Venice: Gli specchi, Marsilio, 1996.

"Amarsi da morire." *L'Espresso,* January 17, 1988. Rome: Archivio Centrale dello Stato, Consoli Archive, Binder 295.

"Controdolore in Casa Sua." *AUT* 26 (September 15, 1974): 35–38. Rome: Archivio Centrale dello Stato, Consoli Archive, Binder 294.

"Conversazione inedita con Dario Bellezza." Roma 1977, with Gabriella Sica. *Nuovi Argomenti.* Edited by Maria Borio. April 30, 2015. http://www.nuovi argomenti.net/poesie/conversazione-inedita-con-dario-bellezza/.

"La condizione di quelli che sono diversi." *Paese Sera,* September 15, 1972. Rome: Archivio Centrale dello Stato, Consoli Archive, Binder 294.

La penultima pagina OMPO, no. 1, aprile 1975, pag. 15. Edited by Massimo Consoli. http://www.culturagay.it/documento/29.

"Per qualcosa in meno dello scandalo." *Paese Sera,* March 18, 1983. Rome: Archivio Centrale dello Stato, Consoli Archive, Binder 295.

"Un mondo senza poesia, gli occhi *di Pino Pelosi." Paese Sera,* May 4, 1976. Rome: Archivio Centrale dello Stato, Consoli Archive, Binder 294.

Other Works

Abelove, Henry, Michèle Aine Barale, and David M. Halperin, eds. *The Lesbian and Gay Studies Reader.* New York: Routledge, 1993.

Azzaro, Angela. "Da Stonewall al Colosseo." *Liberazione,* September 8, 2000, IV, V. Rome: Archivio Centrale dello Stato, Consoli Archive, Binder 295

Baldoni, Luca. "La poesia di Dario Bellezza a dieci anni dalla sua scomparsa." *Italian Poetry Review* 1 (2006): 67–91.

Baldoni, Luca, ed. *Le parole tra gli uomini. Antologia di poesia gay italiana dal Novecento al presente.* Rome: Robin Edizioni, 2012.

Baranski, Zygmunt, and Rebecca J. West, eds. *The Cambridge Companion to Modern Italian Culture.* New York: Cambridge University Press, 2001.

Bassani, Giorgio. *Gli occhiali d'oro.* Turin: Einaudi, 1958.

Bassani, Giorgio. *The Garden of the Finzi-Continis.* Translated by Isabel Quigley. New York: Atheneum Books. 1965.

Bassani, Giorgio. *The Gold-Rimmed Spectacles.* Translated by Isabel Quigley. London: Faber and Faber, 1960.

Bataille, Georges. *Visions of Excess: Selected Writing, 1927–1939.* Edited by Alan Stoekl. Translated by Allan Stoekl with Carl R. Lovitt and Donald M. Leslie Jr. Minneapolis: University of Minnesota Press, 1985.

Berardinelli, Alfonso, and Franco Cordelli, eds. *Il pubblico della poesia.* Rome: Castlevecchi, 2015.

Eernstein, Charles. *Close Listening: Poetry and the Performed Word*. Oxford: Oxford University Press, 1998.

Bersani, Leo. "Is the Rectum a Grave?" *October* 43 (Winter 1987): 197–222.

Bertolucci, Attilio. *Le Poesie*. 1990. Reprint, Milan: Garzanti "I grandi libri," 2014.

Bertolucci, Attilio. *Winter Journey*. Translated by Nicholas Benson. West Lafayette, IN: Parlor Press, 2005.

Borio, Maria. "*Invettive e licenze* e la poesia degli anni Settanta: Analisi di *Il mare di soggettività sto perlustrando* . . . di Dario Bellezza." *Poesia, di Luigia Sorrentino* (blog), August 7, 2015. https://www.luigiasorrentino.it/2015/08/07/maria-borio-dario-bellezza/#more-46417.

Borio, Maria. *Poetiche e individui, La poesia italiana dal 1970 al 2000*. Venice: Marsilio, 2018.

Brock, Geoffrey, ed. *The FSG Book of Twentieth-Century Italian Poetry*. New York: Farrar, Straus and Giroux, 2012.

Buffoni, Franco. *Mario Mieli raccontato da Franco Buffoni*. Wikiradio, November 3, 2017. https://www.youtube.com/watch?v=id8-n5msqDo.

Calabretta-Sadjer, Ryan. *Divergenze in Celluloide: Colore, Migrazione e Identità nei film gay di Ferzan Ozpetek*. Milano: Mimesis/Cinema, 2017.

Calabretta-Sadjer, Ryan, ed. *Pasolini's Lasting Impressions. Death, Eros, and Literary Enterprise in the Opus of Pier Paolo Pasolini*. Madison, Teaneck: Fairleigh Dickinson University Press, 2018.

Carratoni, Velio. "Omaggio a Dario Bellezza: Premio Montale 1994, XII edizione, Relazione finale." *Fermenti*, no. 209 (1994). Consoli Archive, Binder 295.

Cavafy, Constantine. *The Complete Poems of Cavafy*. Translated by Rae Daleven. New York: Harcourt Brace Jovanovich, 1976.

Cavallaro, Fabrizio, ed. *L'arcano fascino dell'amore tradito*. Rome: Giulio Perrone Editore, 2006.

Cestaro, Gary P., ed. *Queer Italia: Same-Sex Desire in Italian Literature and Film*. New York: Palgrave Macmillan, 2004.

Colasanti, Arnaldo. *Dario il grande: La poesia di Dario Bellezza*. Forli: Capire Edizioni, 2019.

Condini, Ned, ed. and trans. *An Anthology of Modern Italian Poetry*. New York: Modern Language Association of America, 2009.

Consoli, Massimo. *Affetti speciali*. Bolsena, VT: R. Massari editore, 1999.

Consoli, Massimo. "C.I.D.A.M.S. Letter, from Massimo Consoli to Dario Bellezza," Rome: Archivio Centrale dello Stato, Consoli Archive, Binder 294, Corrispondenza, "Istituto Italiano di Storia Sociale," January 2, 1974.

Consoli, Massimo. "La Gay House Chiusa dal Comune." *Corriere della Sera*, January 2, 1981. Rome: Archivio Centrale dello Stato: Consoli Archive, Binder 295.

Corriere della Sera. "Il Premio Bolognese di Poesía, Assegnato il 'Gatti': Vincitori Dario Bellezza e Franco Manescalchi." November 28, 1971. Consoli Archive, Binder 294.

Covino, Peter. "Dario Bellezza, Biographical Notes." *Atlanta Review* 27, no. 2 (2011).

Covino, Peter. "Innovation, Interdisciplinarity, and Cultural Exchange in Italian American Poetry." In *Teaching Italian American Literature, Film, and Popular*, edited by Edvige Giunta and Kathleen Zamboni McCormick, 50–61. New York: Modern Language Association, 2010.

Covino, Peter. "Italy." Edited and translated with Chad Davidson and Marella Feltrin-Morris. In *Modern European Poets (1968–2008)*, edited by Wayne Miller and Kevin Prufer, 61–66. Minneapolis: Graywolf, 2008.

Covino, Peter. "Queering an Italian American Poetic Legacy." In *Who's Yer Daddy? Gay Writers Celebrate Their Mentors and Forerunners*, edited by Jim Elledge and David Groff, 212–20. Madison: University of Wisconsin Press, 2012.

Cristallo, Myriam. *Uscir Fuori, Dieci anni di lotte omosessuali in Italia; 1971–1981.* Rome: Sandro Teti editore, 2017.

D'Agostino, Alessandro. "Dario Bellezza, l'ultima intervista al poeta." *Poeti di azione*, June 12, 2015. http://poetidazione.it/blog/news/dario-bellezza-lultima -intervista-del-poeta-esclusivo/#.XPAsoNNKj_Q.

"Dario Bellezza vs. Aldo Busi." *Mixer Cultura*, 1987. YouTube. September 10, 2011, video, 6:42. https://www.youtube.com/watch?v=E7KqBmoQugQ.

Dean, Tim. "Bareback Time." In *Queer Times, Queer Becomings*, edited by E. L. McCallum and Mikko Tuhkanen, 75–99. Albany: State University of New York Press, 2011.

Dean, Tim. "Lacan Meets Queer Theory." In *The Routledge Queer Studies Reader*, edited by Donald E. Hall and Annamarie Jagose, 150–62. Abingdon Oxon: Routledge, 2013.

Deidier, Roberto. "*Tutte le poesie* di Dario Bellezza con Roberto Deidier." Rairadio, *Fahrenheit*, February 23, 2015. http://www.rai.it/dl.

Deleuze, Gilles, and Félix Guattari. *Anti-Oedipus, Capitalism and Schizophrenia*. Translated by Robert Hurley, Mark Seem, and Helen R. Lane. New York: Viking Press, 1977.

Deleuze, Gilles, and Félix Guattari. *L'anti-Edipo, Capitalismo e schizofrenia*. Translated by Alessandro Fontana. Einaudi: Turin, 1975.

Della Rovere, Roberto. "Il fascino oscuro delle 'dark rooms': I gay si dividono." *Corriere della Sera*, May 13, 1993, 47. Rome: Archivio Centrale dello Stato, Consoli Archive, Binder 295.

DiGiacomo, Antonio. "Dario Bellezza al Michelagniolo." *Roma Gay News*, no. 34 (February 14, 1992): 7. Rome: Archivio Centrale dello Stato, Consoli Archive, Binder 295.

Federici, Corrado. "Dario Bellezza." In *Twentieth-Century Italian Poets: Second Series*, edited by Giovanna Wedel De Stasio, Glauco Cambon, and Antonio Illiano, 45–54. Dictionary of Literary Biography 128. Detroit: Gale, 1993.

Feldman, Ruth, and Brian Swan, eds. *Italian Poetry Today*. St. Paul, MN: New Rivers Press, 1979.

Fortunato, Mario. "Vi mando all'inferno" Polemiche / L'ultimo libro di Dario Bellezza. *Panorama*. March 12, 1984. Rome: Archivio Centrale dello Stato, Binder 294.

Foucault, Michel. *La cura di sé*: Storia della sessualità 3. 13th ed. Translated by Laura Guarino. Milan: Feltrinelli Editore, 2016.

Foucault, Michel. *The History of Sexuality*. Vol. 1, *An Introduction*. New York: Random House, 1980.

"Funerali a Roma del poeta Dario Bellezza." Roma, 2 aprile 1996, Foto archivio Circolo Michelangiolo. Accessed February 23, 2024. https://www.youtube .com/watch?v=b82Fl6STdYU.

Giacomo Leopardi. *Canti*. Translated and annotated by Jonathan Galassi. New York: Farrar Straus, and Giroux, 2010.

Ginsberg, Allen. Letter to Dario Bellezza, February 13, 1996, Rome: Archivio dello Stato, Consoli Archive, Adesioni, Binder 297.

Ginsberg, Allen. The Allen Ginsberg Project. Accessed February 29, 2024. https://allenginsberg.org/2012/08/castelporziano/.

Giovanetti, Paolo. *La poesia italiana degli anni duemila. Un percorso di lettura*. Rome: Carocci, 2017.

Gnerre, Francesco. "Ricordo di Dario Bellezza." April 23, 2006. http://www .culturagay.it/saggio/305.

Golino, Enzo. "Palazzeschi." February 18, 2001. https://ricerca.repubblica.it/ repubblica/archivio/repubblica/.

Gregorini, Maurizio. *Il male di Dario Bellezza: vita e morte di un poeta*. Viterbo: Stampa alternativa / Nuovi equilibri, 2006.

Gregorini, Maurizio. *Morte di Bellezza: Storia di una verità nascosta*. Tarquinia: Castelvecchi, 1997.

Hall, Donald E., and Annamarie Jagose, eds. *The Routledge Queer Studies Reader*. Abingdon, Oxon: Routledge, 2013.

Harvey, Keith. "Translating Camp Talk: Gay Identities and Cultural Transfer." In *The Translations Studies Reader*, edited by Lawrence Venuti, 402–22. 2nd ed. London: Routledge, 2004.

Hocquenghem, Guy. *Homosexual Desire*. Translated by Daniella Dangoor. Durham, NC: Duke University Press, 1993.

Holland, Walter. "The Calamus Root: A Study of American Gay Poetry Since World War II." In *Gay and Lesbian Literature since World War II: History and Memory*, edited by Sonya L. Jones, 5–26. New York: Hawthorn Press, 1998.

Inzerillo, Giovanni. *Dalla vita assassinato alla poesie: Il Canzoniere di puro disamore di Dario Bellezza*. Firenze: Franco Cesati Editore, 2019.

Joris, Pierre, and Jerome Rothenberg, eds. *Poems for the Millennium: The University of California Book of Modern and Postmodern Poetry*. Vol. 1, *From Fin-de-Siecle to Negritude*. Berkeley: University of California Press, 1998.

Joris, Pierre, and Jerome Rothenberg, eds. *Poems for the Millennium: The University of California Book of Modern and Postmodern Poetry*. Vol. 2, *From Postwar to the Millennium*. Berkeley, Berkeley: University of California Press, 1998.

Kaufman, Walter. *Nietzsche: Philosopher, Psychologist, Antichrist*. 3rd ed. Princeton, NJ: Princeton University Press, 1968.

Kaufman, Walter. *The Portable Nietzsche*. Translated and edited by Walter Kaufman. New York: Viking Press, 1970.

Kristeva, Julia. *Powers of Horror: An Essay on Abjection*. Translated by Leon S. Roudiez. New York: Columbia University Press, 1982.

La Licata, Francesco. *Storia di Giovanni Falcone*. 5th ed. Milan: Mondadori, Universale Economica, 2006.

Leitch, Vincent B. "Julia Kristeva." In *Norton Anthology of Theory and Criticism*. New York: Norton, 2001.

Lombardi-Diop, Cristina, and Caterina Romeo, eds. *Postcolonial Italy Challenging National Homogeneity*. New York: Palgrave Macmillan, 2012

Massumi, Brian. *A User's Guide to Capitalism and Schizophrenia: Deviations from Deleuze and Guattari*. Cambridge, MA: MIT Press, 1992.

Mieli, Mario. *Homosexuality and Liberation Elements of a Gay Critique*. Translated by David Fernbach. London: Gay Men's Press, 1980.

Miller, Wayne, and Kevin Prufer, eds. *New European Poets 1968–2008*. Minneapolis: Graywolf, 2008.

Minetti, Giulia DiMaria, and Silvia Tortora. "Insulti e grida." *Epoca*, March 13, 1988, 56–59. Rome: Archivio dello Stato, Consoli Archive, Binder 295.

Montale, Eugenio. *Collected Poems 1920–1954*. Translated and annotated by Jonathan Galassi. New York: Farrar, Straus and Giroux, 1998.

Montale, Eugenio. *Satura*. Translated by William Arrowsmith. New York: Norton, 1998.

Montanari, Tomaso. "Barocco: La vertigine di uno stile per sempre contemporaneo." *La Repubblica*, July 8, 2016.

Moravia, Alberto. "Morte Segreta." *Corriere della Sera*, April 17, 1976. Rome: Archivio Centrale dello Stato, Consoli Archive, Binder 293.

Niglio, Francesco. *Dario Bellezza*. Rome: Altrimedia Edizioni, 1999.

Nirenstein, Susanna. "Gay a Monte Caprino? 'È ora di finirla,' Dario Bellezza parla, dei recenti episodi di violenza." *La Repubblica*, September 30, 1984. Consoli Archive, Binder 295.

Orgel, Stephen. "Ganymede Agonistes." *GLQ: A Journal of Lesbian and Gay Studies* 12, no. 3 (2004): 485–501.

Ortese, Anna Maria. *Bellezza, addio. Lettere di Anna Maria Ortese a Dario Bellezza (1972–1992)*. Edited by Adelia Battista. Milan: Archinto, 2011.

Ovid. *Metamorphoses*. Translated by Rolf Humphries. Bloomington: Indiana University Press, 1955.

Palazezzchi, Aldo. *The Arsonist*. Translated by Nicholas Benson. Los Angeles: Otis Books, 2013.

Paris, Enzo. "Dario Bellezza, il poeta maudit." *Il manifesto*, March 30, 2021. https://ilmanifesto.it/dario-bellezza-il-poeta-maudit.

Pasolini, Pier Paolo. *Petrolio*. Translated by Ann Goldstein. New York: Pantheon Books, 1998.

Pasolini, Pier Paolo. *Pier Paolo Pasolini: Poems*. Translated by Norman MacAfee with Luciano Martinengo. 1982. Reprint, New York: Farrar, Straus and Giroux, 1996.

Pasolini, Pier Paolo. *The Selected Poems*. Translated and edited by Stephen Sartarelli. Chicago: University of Chicago Press, 2014.

Perloff, Marjorie. *Differentials: Poetry, Poetics, Pedagogy*. Tuscaloosa: University of Alabama Press, 2004.

Pezzana, Angelo. *Un Omosessuale Normale*. Diario di una ricerca d'identità attraverso il ricordo, la storia, il costume, le vite. Viterbo: Stampa Alternativa / Nuovi Equilibri, 2010.

Piccini, Daniele, ed. *La poesia Italiana dal 1960 a oggi*. Milan: BUR, RCS Libri, 2005.

Priori, Daniele. *Diario di un mostro: Omaggio insolito a Dario Bellezza*. Rome: Albano Laziale, Anemone Purpurea, 2006.

Rizzo, Gianluca. *Poetry on the Stage: The Theatre of the Italian Avant-Garde*. Toronto: University of Toronto Press, 2020.

Rizzo, Marta. "Bellezza addio: lo scandalo come responsabilità. Intervista a Carmen Giardina." *Articolo 21*, February 17, 2024. https://www.articolo21.org/2024/02/bellezza-addio-lo-scandalo-come-responsabilita-intervista-a-carmen-giardina/.

Roach, Tom. *Friendship as a Way of Life: Foucault, AIDS, and the Politics of Shared Estrangement*. Albany: State University of New York Press, 2012.

Rosselli, Amelia. *War Variations*. Translated by Paul Vangelisti. Los Angeles: Green Integer, 2005.

Rosselli, Amelia. *Locomotrix: Selected Poetry and Prose of Amelia Rosselli*. Translated and edited by Jennifer Scappettone. Chicago: University of Chicago Press, 2012.

Ruberto, Laura, and Joseph Sciorra, eds. *New Italian Migration to the United States*. Vol. 1. Urbana: University of Illinois Press, 2017.

Sardina, Massimiliano. "L'amore baldracco: La Bellezza di Dario. Vita e opera di Dario Bellezza." *Amedit*, no. 30 (March 2017): 12–17.

Sica, Luciana. "Dario Bellezza, Il mio addio alla vita." *La Repubblica*, February 21, 1996. https://ricerca.repubblica.it/repubblica/archivio/repubblica/.

Siciliano, Enzo. "Amor di poeti." *La Stampa* 105, no. 151 (July 2, 1971). Rome: Archivio Centrale dello Stato, Consoli Archive, Binder 294. http://www.archiviolastampa.it/.

Tanner, Henry. "Moro Slain, Body Found in Rome." *New York Times*, May 10, 1978.

Testa, Enrico, ed. *Dopo la lirica: Poeti Italiani 1960–2000*. Turin: Giulio Einaudi, 2005.

Toni, Alberto. "L'unica trasgressione è la castità. Eros e letteratura Parla Dario Bellezza." *Paese Sera*, March 9, 1988. Rome: Archivio Centrale dello Stato, Consoli Archive, Binder 294.

Tuck, Lily. *Woman of Rome: A Life of Elsa Morante*. New York: Harper Collins, 2008.

Veneziani, Antonio. *Addio amori, addio cuori: Dario Bellezza*. Rome: Fermenti, Rivista di critica del costume and della cultura, 1996.

Venuti, Lawrence. *Translation Changes Everything*. London: Routledge, 2013.

Venuti, Lawrence, ed. *The Translation Studies Reader*. 2nd ed. London: Routledge, 2004.

Virgil. *Georgics*. Translated by Smith Palmer Bovie. Chicago: University of Chicago Press, 1966.

Wardal, Count Federico. "Perturbation Premiere by Dario Bellezza, Starring Count Federico Wardal on Pasolini Integral Version." January 23, 2020. https://www.youtube.com/watch?v=MStfj1wNkSs.

Zappalà, Giuseppe Leonardo. "'Mia parte ctonia femminile': Amelia Rosselli nell'opera di Dario Bellezza." *Quaderni del '900*, no. 16 (November 16, 2016): 27–38.

Zecchi, Simona. *Pasolini, massacro di un poeta*. Milan: Adriano Salani Editore, 2015.

DARIO BELLEZZA (1944–96) was Italy's first openly gay, major prize-winning poet-novelist-playwright, who died a premature death of AIDS-related complications. Over the course of a twenty-five-year career, he published more than twenty books, including eight full-length poetry collections, eight novels, two plays, translations from the French, and nonfiction. Twentieth-century Italian and American literary luminaries Pier Paolo Pasolini, Alberto Moravia, Elsa Morante, Gregory Corso, and Allen Ginsberg, among others, championed his work. Significantly, Bellezza's literary career extends two decades beyond Pasolini's death, and he embraced his identity as an out gay man in an era of increased polemicizing of gay rights and harsh opposition by the Vatican. The sheer variety of forms, from epigram to brash love-lyric to sustained political narrative, coupled with the fervor of Bellezza's voice make a compelling argument for his lasting importance among the best poets of the second half of the twentieth century.

PETER COVINO's translation work has been awarded fellowships from the National Endowment for the Arts and the Richmond American International University of London, Rome Programme. After a fourteen-year career as a social worker in the fields of AIDS services and foster care, Covino is an associate professor of English in the PhD Program at the University of Rhode Island, specializing in contemporary poetry, translation, and ethnic studies. He is also a well-published scholar, poet, editor, and author, with works that include a coedited essay collection on Italian American literature and the prize-winning poetry books *The Right Place to Jump* and *Cut Off the Ears of Winter* (2007 PEN-American Osterweil Award). Covino is the founding editor and faculty advisor of the *Ocean State Review*, and since 1998 a founding editor-trustee of the nonprofit press Barrow Street Inc.

WISCONSIN POETRY SERIES

Sean Bishop and Jesse Lee Kercheval, series editors
Ronald Wallace, founding series editor

How the End First Showed (B) • D. M. Aderibigbe

New Jersey (B) • Betsy Andrews

Salt (B) • Renée Ashley

(At) Wrist (B) • Tacey M. Atsitty

Horizon Note (B) • Robin Behn

What Sex Is Death? (T) • Dario Bellezza, selected and translated by
  Peter Covino

About Crows (FP) • Craig Blais

Mrs. Dumpty (FP) • Chana Bloch

Shopping, or The End of Time (FP) • Emily Bludworth de Barrios

The Declarable Future (4L) • Jennifer Boyden

The Mouths of Grazing Things (B) • Jennifer Boyden

Help Is on the Way (4L) • John Brehm

No Day at the Beach • John Brehm

Sea of Faith (B) • John Brehm

Reunion (FP) • Fleda Brown

Brief Landing on the Earth's Surface (B) • Juanita Brunk

Ejo: Poems, Rwanda, 1991–1994 (FP) • Derick Burleson

Grace Engine • Joshua Burton

The Roof of the Whale Poems (T) • Juan Calzadilla, translated by
  Katherine M. Hedeen and Olivia Lott

Jagged with Love (B) • Susanna Childress

Almost Nothing to Be Scared Of (4L) • David Clewell

(B) = Winner of the Brittingham Prize in Poetry
(FP) = Winner of the Felix Pollak Prize in Poetry
(4L) = Winner of the Four Lakes Prize in Poetry
(T) = Winner of the Wisconsin Prize for Poetry in Translation